Also by Rhonda Byrne

The Secret

The Secret Gratitude Book

The Secret Daily Teachings

The Power

The Magic

Hero

How The Secret *Changed My Life*

Also from The Secret

The Secret to Teen Power
by Paul Harrington

The Power of Henry's Imagination
by Skye Byrne and Nic George

The Secret

10th Anniversary Edition

Rhonda Byrne

SIMON & SCHUSTER

London · New York · Sydney · Toronto · New Delhi

BEYOND WORDS

Hillsboro, Oregon

First published in Great Britain by Simon & Schuster UK Ltd, 2016

15

Simon & Schuster UK Ltd
1st Floor, 222 Gray's Inn Road
London WC1X 8HB

www.simonandschuster.co.uk
www.simonandschuster.com.au
www.simonandschuster.co.in

Simon & Schuster Australia, Sydney
Simon & Schuster India, New Delhi

Originally published in the US by Atria, an imprint of Simon & Schuster, Inc.
1230 Avenue of the Americas, New York, NY 10020

The information contained in this book is intended to be educational and not for diagnosis, prescription or treatment of any health disorders or as a substitute for financial planning. This information should not replace consultation with a competent healthcare or financial professional. The content of this book is intended to be used as an adjunct to a rational and responsible programme prescribed by a healthcare practitioner or financial professional. The author and publisher are in no way liable for any misuse of the material. .

Book design by Gozer Media P/L (Australia) gozer.com.au, directed by Nic George & The Secret
10th Anniversary Edition cover design by Nic George for The Secret, and Albert Tang, art director for Atria Books

A CIP catalogue record for this book is available from the British Library

Hardback ISBN: 978-1-84737-029-7
eBook ISBN: 978-1-84739-618-1
Paperback ISBN: 978-1-4711-7239-7

Printed and bound in India by Replika Press Pvt. Ltd.

MIX
Paper from
responsible sources
FSC® C016779
FSC
www.fsc.org

As above, so below.
As within, so without.

—*The Emerald Tablet,* circa 3000 BC

Dedicated to You

May The Secret bring you love and
joy for your entire existence.

That is my intention for you,
and for the world.

Contents

Foreword to the 10th Anniversary Edition

After ten years of living The Secret, practicing it daily, and observing it operating in every possible life situation, I've come to understand this most powerful law at a far deeper level. When used correctly, I have experienced the law of attraction lifting me up to incredible heights, and when used in error, I have experienced the full repercussions. But in every situation the law of attraction remained unfailingly consistent in its response, and it does so not just for me, but for every one of us.

In celebration of The Secret's 10th Anniversary, I want to share the ten most life-changing insights I have had over the last ten years of practicing and living The Secret every day. These ten insights expand on the knowledge already contained in this book, but, if studied repeatedly and carefully practiced, they will make manifesting your desires easier than ever before, eliminate struggles and suffering, and above all will give you the opportunity to reach a level of peace and joy that you might never have felt before.

You'll find these ten insights in the Afterword at the end of this book.

Over the last decade I have come to know one thing with the most certainty: the only thing standing between us and a life filled with joy and everything we want is our very own self!

With gratitude,

Rhonda

Foreword

A year ago, my life had collapsed around me. I'd worked myself into exhaustion, my father died suddenly, and my relationships with my work colleagues and loved ones were in turmoil. Little did I know at the time, out of my greatest despair was to come the greatest gift.

I'd been given a glimpse of a Great Secret—The Secret to life. The glimpse came in a hundred-year-old book, given to me by my daughter Hayley. I began tracing The Secret back through history. I couldn't believe all the people who knew this. They were the greatest people in history: Plato, Shakespeare, Newton, Hugo, Beethoven, Lincoln, Emerson, Edison, Einstein.

Incredulous, I asked, "Why doesn't *everyone* know this?" A burning desire to share The Secret with the world consumed me, and I began searching for people alive today who knew The Secret.

One by one they began to emerge. I became a magnet: as I began to search, one great living master after another was drawn to me.

When I discovered one teacher, that one would link to the next, in a perfect chain. If I was on the wrong track, something else would catch my attention, and through the diversion the next great teacher would appear. If I "accidentally" pressed the wrong link on an Internet search, I would be led to a vital piece of information. In a few short weeks I had traced The Secret back through the centuries, and I had discovered the modern-day practitioners of the Secret.

The vision of taking The Secret to the world in a film had become fixed in my mind, and over the following two months my film and television production team learned The Secret. It was imperative that every team member knew it, because without its knowledge, what we were about to attempt would be impossible.

We did not have a single teacher secured to film, but we knew The Secret, and so with utter faith I flew from Australia to the United States where the majority of the teachers were based. Seven weeks later The Secret team had filmed fifty-five of the greatest teachers across the United States, with over 120 hours of film. With every step, with every breath, we used The Secret to create the *The Secret*. We literally magnetized everything and everyone to us. Eight months later *The Secret* was released.

As the film swept the world, stories of miracles began to flood in: people wrote about healing from chronic pain, depression, and disease; walking for the first time after an accident; even recovering from a deathbed. We have received thousands of accounts of The Secret being used to bring about large sums of money and unexpected checks in the mail. People have used The Secret to manifest their perfect homes, life partners, cars, jobs, and promotions, with many accounts of businesses being transformed within days of applying The Secret. There have been heart-warming stories of stressed relationships involving children being restored to harmony.

Some of the most magnificent stories we have received have come from children using The Secret to attract what they want, including high grades and friends. The Secret has inspired doctors to share the knowledge with their patients; universities and schools with their students; health clubs with their clients; churches of all denominations and spiritual centers with their congregations. There are Secret parties being held in homes around the world, as people share the knowledge with loved ones and families. The Secret has been used to attract all manner of things—from a specific feather to ten million dollars. All of this has taken place in the few months since the release of the film.

My intention in creating *The Secret* was—and still is—that it will bring joy to billions around the world. The Secret team is experiencing the realization of that intention every day, as we receive thousands upon thousands of letters from people across the world, of all ages, all races, and all nationalities, expressing gratitude for the joy of The Secret. There isn't a single thing that you cannot do with this knowledge. It doesn't matter who you are or where you are, The Secret can give you whatever you want.

Twenty-four amazing teachers are featured in this book. Their words were filmed all over the United States, all at different times, yet they speak as one voice. This book contains The Secret teachers' words, and it also contains miraculous stories of The Secret in action. I have shared all of the easy paths, tips, and shortcuts that I have learned so that you can live the life of your dreams.

You will notice throughout the book that in certain places I have capitalized the word "You." The reason I did this is because I want you, the reader, to feel and know that I created this book for you. I am speaking to you personally when I say You. My intention is for you to feel a personal connection with these pages, because The Secret has been created for You.

As you travel through its pages and you learn The Secret, you will come to know how you can have, be, or do anything you want. You will come to know who you really are. You will come to know the true magnificence that awaits you.

Acknowledgments

With the deepest gratitude I wish to thank every person who has come into my life and inspired, touched, and illuminated me through their presence.

I would also like to acknowledge and express my gratitude to the following people for their magnificent support and contributions to my journey and to the creation of this book:

For generously sharing their wisdom, love, and divinity, I pay homage to the featured co-authors of *The Secret*: John Assaraf, Michael Bernard Beckwith, Lee Brower, Jack Canfield, Dr. John Demartini, Marie Diamond, Mike Dooley, Bob Doyle, Hale Dwoskin, Morris Goodman, Dr. John Gray, Dr. John Hagelin, Bill Harris, Dr. Ben Johnson, Loral Langemeier, Lisa Nichols, Bob Proctor, James Ray, David Schirmer, Marci Shimoff, Dr. Joe Vitale, Dr. Denis Waitley, Neale Donald Walsch, and Dr. Fred Alan Wolf.

The magnificent human beings that make up *The Secret* production team: Paul Harrington, Glenda Bell, Skye Byrne, and Nic George.

Also to Drew Heriot, Daniel Kerr, Damian Corboy, and to all who journeyed with us in the creation of the film *The Secret*.

Gozer Media, for the creation of the superb graphics and for impregnating them with the feeling of The Secret: James Armstrong, Shamus Hoare, and Andy Lewis.

The CEO of The Secret, Bob Rainone, who was delivered to us from heaven.

Michael Gardiner and the legal and advisory team across Australia and the United States.

The Secret website team: Dan Hollings, John Herren, and all at Powerful Intentions who manage and run The Secret Forum, along with the wonderful people on the forum.

The great avatars and master teachers from the past, whose writings lit a burning fire of desire within me. I have walked in the shadows of their greatness, and I honor every one of them. Special thanks to Robert Collier and Robert Collier Publications, Wallace Wattles, Charles Haanel, Joseph Campbell and the Joseph Campbell Foundation, Prentice Mulford, Genevieve Behrend, and Charles Fillmore.

To Richard Cohn and Cynthia Black of Atria Books/Beyond Words, and Judith Curr of Simon & Schuster, for opening their hearts and embracing The Secret. For their editing: Henry Covi and Julie Steigerwaldt.

For their generosity in sharing their stories: Cathy Goodman; Susan Sloate and her son Colin Halm; Susan Morrice, director of Belize Natural Energy; Jeannie MacKay; and Joe Sugarman.

For their inspirational teachings: Dr. Robert Anthony, Jerry and Esther Hicks and the teachings of Abraham, David Cameron Gikandi, John Harricharan, Catherine Ponder, Gay and Katie Hendricks, Stephen MR Covey, Eckhart Tolle, and Debbie Ford. For their generous support: Chris and Janet Attwood, Marcia Martin, members of the Transformational Leaders Council, the Spiritual Cinema Circle, the staff at Agape Spiritual Center, and the assistants and staff of all the teachers featured in *The Secret*.

My precious friends for their love and support: Marcy Koltun-Crilley, Margaret Rainone, Athena Golianis and John Walker, Elaine Bate, Andrea Keir, and Michael and Kendra Abay. And my amazing family: Peter Byrne; my very special sisters: Jan Child for her invaluable help with this book, Pauline Vernon, Kaye Izon (deceased), and Glenda Bell, who is always by my side and whose love and support knows no limits. My courageous and beautiful mother, Irene Izon, and in memory of my father, Ronald Izon, whose light and love continue to shine through our lives.

And finally to my daughters, Hayley and Skye Byrne. To Hayley, who was responsible for the beginning of my life and its true journey, and to Skye, who followed my footsteps in the creation of this book, and who brilliantly edited and transformed my words. My daughters are the precious jewels of my life, and they illuminate every breath I take through their very existence.

The Secret Revealed

BOB PROCTOR
PHILOSOPHER, AUTHOR, AND PERSONAL COACH
The Secret gives you anything you want: happiness, health, and wealth.

DR. JOE VITALE
METAPHYSICIAN, MARKETING SPECIALIST, AND AUTHOR
You can have, do, or be anything you want.

JOHN ASSARAF
ENTREPRENEUR AND MONEYMAKING EXPERT
We can have whatever it is that we choose. I don't care how big it is.

*What kind of a house do you want to live in? Do you want
to be a millionaire? What kind of a business do you want to
have? Do you want more success? What do you really want?*

DR. JOHN DEMARTINI
PHILOSOPHER, CHIROPRACTOR, HEALER, AND
PERSONAL TRANSFORMATION SPECIALIST
This is the Great Secret of Life.

DR. DENIS WAITLEY
PSYCHOLOGIST AND TRAINER IN THE FIELD OF
MIND POTENTIAL
*The leaders in the past who had The Secret wanted
to keep the power and not share the power. They kept
people ignorant of The Secret. People went to work, they
did their job, they came home. They were on a treadmill with
no power, because The Secret was kept in the few.*

Throughout history there have been many who coveted the knowledge of The Secret, and there have been many who found a way of
spreading this knowledge to the world.

MICHAEL BERNARD BECKWITH
VISIONARY AND FOUNDER OF AGAPE
INTERNATIONAL SPIRITUAL CENTER
I've seen many miracles take place in people's lives.

Financial miracles, miracles of physical healing, mental healing, healing of relationships.

JACK CANFIELD
AUTHOR, TEACHER, LIFE COACH, AND MOTIVATIONAL SPEAKER

All of this happened because of knowing how to apply The Secret.

What Is The Secret?

BOB PROCTOR

You've probably been sitting there wondering, "What is The Secret?" I'll tell you how I've come to understand it.

We all work with one infinite power. We all guide ourselves by exactly the same laws. The natural laws of the universe are so precise that we don't even have any difficulty building spaceships, we can send people to the moon, and we can time the landing with the precision of a fraction of a second.

Wherever you are—India, Australia, New Zealand, Stockholm, London, Toronto, Montreal, or New York—we're all working with one power. One Law. It's attraction!

The Secret is the law of attraction!

*Everything that's coming into your life you are attracting
into your life. And it's attracted to you by virtue of the images
you're holding in your mind.* It's what you're thinking.
Whatever is going on in your mind you are attracting to you.

"Every thought of yours is a real thing—a force."

Prentice Mulford (1834–1891)

The greatest teachers who have ever lived have told us that the law
of attraction is the most powerful law in the Universe.

Poets such as William Shakespeare, Robert Browning, and William
Blake delivered it in their poetry. Musicians such as Ludwig van
Beethoven expressed it through their music. Artists such as Leo-
nardo da Vinci depicted it in their paintings. Great thinkers including Socrates, Plato, Ralph Waldo Emerson, Pythagoras, Sir Francis
Bacon, Sir Isaac Newton, Johann Wolfgang von Goethe, and Victor
Hugo shared it in their writings and teachings. Their names have
been immortalized, and their legendary existence has survived
centuries.

Religions, such as Hinduism, Hermetic traditions, Buddhism,
Judaism, Christianity, and Islam, and civilizations, such as the
ancient Babylonians and Egyptians, delivered it through their writings and stories. Recorded throughout the ages in all its forms, the

law can be found in ancient writings through all the centuries. It was recorded in stone in 3000 BC. Even though some coveted this knowledge, and indeed they did, it has always been there for anyone to discover.

The law began at the beginning of time. It has always been and will always be.

It is the law that determines the complete order in the Universe, every moment of your life, and every single thing you experience in your life. It doesn't matter who you are or where you are, the law of attraction is forming your entire life experience, and this all-powerful law is doing that through your thoughts. You are the one who calls the law of attraction into action, and you do it through your thoughts.

In 1912 Charles Haanel described the law of attraction as "the greatest and the most infallible law upon which the entire system of creation depends."

BOB PROCTOR

Wise people have always known this. You can go right back to the ancient Babylonians. They've always known this. It's a small select group of people.

The ancient Babylonians and their great prosperity have been well documented by scholars. They are also known for creating one of the Seven Wonders of the World, the Hanging Gardens of Babylon. Through their understanding and application of the laws of the Universe, they became one of the wealthiest races in history.

BOB PROCTOR

Why do you think that 1 percent of the population earns around 96 percent of all the money that's being earned? Do you think that's an accident? It's designed that way. They understand something. They understand The Secret, and now you are being introduced to The Secret.

People who have drawn wealth into their lives used The Secret, whether consciously or unconsciously. They think thoughts of abundance and wealth, and they do not allow any contradictory thoughts to take root in their minds. Their predominant thoughts are of wealth. They only *know* wealth, and nothing else exists in their minds. Whether they are aware of it or not, their predominant thoughts of wealth are what brought wealth to them. It is the law of attraction in action.

A perfect example to demonstrate The Secret and the law of attraction in action is this: You may know of people who acquired massive wealth, lost it all, and within a short time acquired massive wealth again. What happened in these cases, whether they knew it or not, is that their dominant thoughts were on wealth; that is how they acquired it in the first instance. Then they allowed fearful thoughts of losing the wealth to enter their minds, until those fearful thoughts of loss became their dominant thoughts. They tipped the scales from thinking thoughts of wealth to thinking thoughts of loss, and so they lost it all. Once they had lost it however, the fear of loss disappeared, and they tipped the scales back with dominant thoughts of wealth. And wealth returned.

The law responds to your thoughts, no matter what they may be.

Like Attracts Like

JOHN ASSARAF

The simplest way for me to look at the law of attraction is if I think of myself as a magnet, and I know that a magnet will attract to it.

You are the most powerful magnet in the Universe! You contain a magnetic power within you that is more powerful than anything in this world, and this unfathomable magnetic power is emitted through your thoughts.

BOB DOYLE
AUTHOR AND LAW OF ATTRACTION SPECIALIST

Basically put, the law of attraction says that like attracts like. But we're really talking at a level of thought.

The law of attraction says *like attracts like,* and so as you think a thought, you are also attracting *like* thoughts to you. Here are more examples you may have experienced of the law of attraction in your life:

Have you ever started to think about something you were not happy about, and the more you thought about it the worse it seemed? That's because as you think one sustained thought, the law of attraction immediately brings more *like* thoughts to you. In a matter of minutes, you have gotten so many *like* unhappy thoughts coming to you that the situation seems to be getting worse. The more you think about it, the more upset you get.

You may have experienced attracting *like* thoughts when you listened to a song, and then found that you couldn't get that song out of your head. The song just kept playing over and over in your mind. When you listened to that song, even though you may not have realized it, you gave your full attention and focus of thought to it. As you did that, you were powerfully attracting more *like* thoughts of that song, and so the law of attraction moved into action and delivered more thoughts of that song, over and over again.

JOHN ASSARAF

Our job as humans is to hold on to the thoughts of what we want, make it absolutely clear in our minds what we want, and from that we start to invoke one of the greatest laws in the Universe, and that's the law of attraction. You become what you think about most, but you also attract what you think about most.

Your life right now is a reflection of your past thoughts. That includes all the great things, and all the things you consider not so great. Since you attract to you what you think about most, it is easy to see what your dominant thoughts have been on every subject of your life, because that is what you have experienced. Until now! Now you are learning The Secret, and with this knowledge, you can change everything.

BOB PROCTOR

If you see it in your mind, you're going to hold it in your hand.

If you can think about what you want in your mind, and make that your dominant thought, you *will* bring it into your life.

MIKE DOOLEY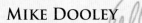

AUTHOR AND INTERNATIONAL SPEAKER

And that principle can be summed up in three simple words. Thoughts become things!

Through this most powerful law, your thoughts become the things in your life. Your thoughts become things! Say this over to yourself and let it seep into your consciousness and your awareness. Your thoughts become things!

JOHN ASSARAF

What most people don't understand is that a thought has a frequency. We can measure a thought. And so if you're thinking that thought over and over and over again, if you're imagining in your mind having that brand new car, having the money that you need, building that company, finding your soul mate . . . if you're imagining what that looks like, you're emitting that frequency on a consistent basis.

DR. JOE VITALE
Thoughts are sending out that magnetic signal that is drawing the parallel back to you.

> "The predominant thought or the mental attitude is the magnet, and the law is that like attracts like, consequently, the mental attitude will invariably attract such conditions as correspond to its nature."

Charles Haanel (1866–1949)

Thoughts are magnetic, and thoughts have a frequency. As you think, those thoughts are sent out into the Universe, and they magnetically attract all *like* things that are on the same frequency. Everything sent out returns to the source. And that source is You.

Think of it this way: we understand that a television station's transmission tower broadcasts via a frequency, which is transformed into pictures on your television. Most of us don't really understand how it works, but we know that each channel has a frequency, and when we tune into that frequency we see the pictures on our television. We choose the frequency by selecting the channel, and we then receive the pictures broadcast on that channel. If we want to see different pictures on our television, we change the channel and tune into a new frequency.

You are a *human* transmission tower, and you are more powerful than any television tower created on earth. You are the most powerful transmission tower in the Universe. Your transmission creates your life and it creates the world. The frequency you transmit reaches beyond cities, beyond countries, beyond the world. It reverberates throughout the entire Universe. And you are transmitting that frequency *with your thoughts*!

The pictures you receive from the transmission of your thoughts are not on a television screen in your living room, they are the pictures of your *life*! Your thoughts create the frequency, they attract *like* things on that frequency, and then they are broadcast back to you as your life pictures. If you want to change anything in your life, change the channel and change the frequency by changing your thoughts.

> "The vibrations of mental forces are the finest and consequently the most powerful in existence."
>
> *Charles Haanel*

BOB PROCTOR

See yourself living in abundance and you will attract it. It works every time, with every person.

As you think of yourself living in abundance, you are powerfully and consciously determining your life through the law of attraction. It's that easy. But then the most obvious question becomes, "Why isn't everybody living the life of their dreams?"

Attract the Good Instead of the Bad

JOHN ASSARAF

Here's the problem. Most people are thinking about what they don't want, and they're wondering why it shows up over and over again.

The only reason why people do not have what they want is because they are thinking more about what they *don't* want than what they *do* want. Listen to your thoughts, and listen to the words you are saying. The law is absolute and there are no mistakes.

An epidemic worse than any plague that humankind has ever seen has been raging for centuries. It is the "don't want" epidemic.

People keep this epidemic alive when they predominantly think, speak, act, and focus on what they "don't want." But this is the generation that will change history, because we are receiving the knowledge that can free us of this epidemic! It begins with you, and you can become a pioneer of this new thought movement by simply thinking and speaking about what you want.

BOB DOYLE

The law of attraction doesn't care whether you perceive something to be good or bad, or whether you don't want it or whether you do want it. It's responding to your thoughts. So if you're looking at a mountain of debt, feeling terrible about it, that's the signal you're putting out into the Universe. "I feel really bad because of all this debt I've got." You're just affirming it to yourself. You feel it on every level of your being. That's what you're going to get more of.

The law of attraction is a law of nature. It is impersonal and it does not see good things or bad things. It is receiving your thoughts and reflecting back to you those thoughts as your life experience. The law of attraction simply gives you whatever it is you are thinking about.

LISA NICHOLS

AUTHOR AND PERSONAL EMPOWERMENT ADVOCATE

The law of attraction is really obedient. When you think of the things that you want, and you focus on them with all of your intention, then the law of attraction will give you exactly what you want, every time. When you focus on the things that you don't want — "I don't want to be late, I don't want to be late" — the law of attraction doesn't hear that you don't want it. It manifests the things that you're thinking of, and so it's going to show up over and over and over again. The law of attraction is not biased to wants or don't wants. When you focus on something, no matter what it happens to be, you really are calling that into existence.

When you focus your thoughts on something you want, and you hold that focus, you are in that moment summoning what you want with the mightiest power in the Universe. The law of attraction doesn't compute "don't" or "not" or "no," or any other words of negation. As you speak words of negation, this is what the law of attraction is receiving:

"I don't want to spill something on this outfit."
> *"I want to spill something on this outfit and I want to spill more things."*

"I don't want a bad haircut."
> *"I want bad haircuts."*

"I don't want to be delayed."
> *"I want delays."*

"I don't want that person to be rude to me."
> *"I want that person and more people to be rude to me."*

"I don't want the restaurant to give away our table."
> *"I want restaurants to give away our tables."*

"I don't want these shoes to hurt."

> *"I want shoes to hurt."*

"I can't handle all this work."

> *"I want more work than I can handle."*

"I don't want to catch the flu."

> *"I want the flu and I want to catch more things."*

"I don't want to argue."

> *"I want more arguing."*

"Don't speak to me like that."

> *"I want you to speak to me like that and I want other people to speak to me like that."*

The law of attraction is giving you what you are thinking about —period!

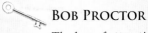

BOB PROCTOR

> *The law of attraction is always working, whether you believe it or understand it or not.*

The law of attraction is the law of creation. Quantum physicists tell us that the entire Universe emerged from thought! You create your life through your thoughts and the law of attraction, and every single person does the same. It doesn't just work if you know about it. It has always been working in your life and every other person's life throughout history. When you become *aware* of this great law, then you become *aware* of how incredibly powerful you are, to be able to THINK your life into existence.

LISA NICHOLS

It's working as much as you're thinking. Any time your thoughts are flowing, the law of attraction is working. When you're thinking about the past, the law of attraction's working. When you're thinking about the present or the future, the law of attraction is working. It's an ongoing process. You don't press pause, you don't press stop. It is forever in action, as your thoughts are.

Whether we realize it or not, we are thinking most of the time. If you are speaking or listening to someone, you are thinking. If you are reading the newspaper or watching television, you are thinking. When you recall memories from your past, you are thinking. When you are considering something in your future, you are thinking. When you are driving, you are thinking. When you are getting ready in the morning, you are thinking. For many of us, the only time we are not thinking is when we are asleep; however, the forces of attraction are still operating on our last thoughts as we fall asleep. Make your last thoughts before going to sleep good thoughts.

MICHAEL BERNARD BECKWITH

Creation is always happening. Every time an individual has a thought, or a prolonged chronic way of thinking, they're in the creation process. Something is going to manifest out of those thoughts.

What you are thinking now is creating your future life. You create your life with your thoughts. Because you are always thinking, you are always creating. What you think about the most or focus on the most, is what will appear as your life.

Like all the laws of nature, there is utter perfection in this law. You create your life. Whatever you sow, you reap! Your thoughts are seeds, and the harvest you reap will depend on the seeds you plant.

If you are complaining, the law of attraction will powerfully bring into your life more situations for you to complain about. If you are listening to someone else complain and focusing on that, sympathizing with them, agreeing with them, in that moment, you are attracting more situations to yourself to complain about.

The law is simply reflecting and giving back to you exactly what you are focusing on with your thoughts. With this powerful knowledge, you can completely change every circumstance and event in your entire life, by changing the way you think.

BILL HARRIS

TEACHER AND FOUNDER OF CENTERPOINTE RESEARCH INSTITUTE

I had a student named Robert, who was taking an online course I have, part of which entails email access to me.

Robert was gay. He outlined all of the grim realities of his life in his emails to me. In his job, his coworkers ganged up on him. It was constantly stressful because of how nasty they were with him. When he walked down the street, he was accosted by homophobic people who wanted to abuse him in some way. He wanted to become a stand-up comedian, and when he did a stand-up comedy job, everybody heckled him about being gay. His whole life was one of unhappiness and misery, and it all focused around being attacked because he was gay.

I began to teach him that he was focusing on what he did not want. I directed him back to his email that he sent me and said, "Read it again. Look at all the things you do not want that you're telling me about. I can tell you're very passionate about this and when you focus on something with a lot of passion, it makes it happen even faster!"

Then he started taking this thing about focusing on what you want to heart, and he began really trying it. What happened within the next six to eight weeks was an absolute miracle. All the people in his office who had been harassing him either transferred to another department, quit working at the company, or started completely leaving him alone. He began to love his job. When he walked down the street, nobody harassed him anymore. They just weren't there. When he did his stand-up comedy routines he started getting standing ovations, and nobody was heckling him!

His whole life changed because he changed from focusing on what he did not want, what he was afraid of, what he wanted to avoid, to focusing on what he did want.

Robert's life changed because he changed his thoughts. He emitted a different frequency out into the Universe. The Universe *must* deliver the pictures of the new frequency, no matter how impossible the situation might seem. Robert's new thoughts became his new frequency, and the pictures of his entire life changed.

Your life is in your hands. No matter where you are now, no matter what has happened in your life, you can begin to consciously choose your thoughts, and you can change your life. There is no such thing as a hopeless situation. Every single circumstance of your life can change!

The Power of Your Mind

 MICHAEL BERNARD BECKWITH

You attract to you the predominant thoughts that you're holding in your awareness, whether those thoughts are conscious or unconscious. That's the rub.

Whether you have been aware of your thoughts in the past or not, *now* you are becoming aware. Right now, with the knowledge of The Secret, you are waking up from a deep sleep and becoming aware! Aware of the knowledge, aware of the law, aware of the power you have through your thoughts.

DR. JOHN DEMARTINI

If you look very carefully when it comes to The Secret, and the power of our mind and the power of our intention in our daily lives, it's all around us. All we have to do is open our eyes and look.

LISA NICHOLS

You can see the law of attraction everywhere. You draw everything to yourself. The people, the job, the circumstances, the health, the wealth, the debt, the joy, the car that you drive, the community that you're in. And you've drawn them all to you, like a magnet. What you think about you bring about. Your whole life is a manifestation of the thoughts that go on in your head.

This is a Universe of inclusion, not exclusion. Nothing is excluded from the law of attraction. Your life is a mirror of the dominant thoughts you think. All living things on this planet operate through the law of attraction. The difference with humans is that they have a mind that can discern. They can use their free will to *choose* their thoughts. They have the power to intentionally think and create their entire life with their mind.

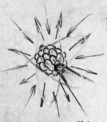

DR. FRED ALAN WOLF

QUANTUM PHYSICIST, LECTURER, AND AWARD-WINNING AUTHOR

I'm not talking to you from the point of view of wishful thinking or imaginary craziness. I'm talking to you from a deeper, basic understanding.

Quantum physics really begins to point to this discovery. It
says that you can't have a Universe without mind entering
into it, and that the mind is actually shaping the very thing
that is being perceived.

If you think about the analogy of being the most powerful transmission tower in the Universe, you will see the perfect correlation
with Dr. Wolf's words. Your mind thinks thoughts and the pictures
are broadcast back as your life experience. You not only create your
life with your thoughts, but your thoughts add powerfully to the
creation of the world. If you thought that you were insignificant
and had no power in this world, think again. Your mind is actually
shaping the world around you.

The amazing work and discoveries of the quantum physicists
over the last eighty years has brought us to a greater understanding of the unfathomable power of the human mind to create.
Their work parallels the words of the world's great minds, including Carnegie, Emerson, Shakespeare, Bacon, Krishna, and
Buddha.

BOB PROCTOR

If you don't understand the law that doesn't mean you should
reject it. You may not understand electricity, and yet you
enjoy the benefits of it. I don't know how it works. But I do
know this: You can cook a man's dinner with electricity, and
you can also cook the man!

MICHAEL BERNARD BECKWITH

Oftentimes when people begin to understand the Great Secret, they become frightened of all the negative thoughts that they have. They need to be aware that it has been scientifically proven that an affirmative thought is hundreds of times more powerful than a negative thought. That eliminates a degree of worry right there.

It really does take many negative thoughts and persistent negative thinking to bring something negative into your life. However, if you persist in thinking negative thoughts over a period of time, they *will* appear in your life. If you worry about having negative thoughts, you will attract more worrying about your negative thoughts, and multiply them at the same time. Decide right now that you are going to think only good thoughts. At the same time, proclaim to the Universe that all your good thoughts are powerful, and that any negative thoughts are weak.

LISA NICHOLS

Thank God that there's a time delay, that all of your thoughts don't come true instantly. We'd be in trouble if they did. The element of time delay serves you. It allows you to reassess, to think about what you want, and to make a new choice.

All of your power to create your life is available right now, because right now is when you are thinking. If you have had some thoughts that will not be beneficial when they manifest, then right now you can change your thinking. You can erase your previous thoughts by replacing them with good thoughts. Time serves you because you can think new thoughts and emit a new frequency, *now*!

DR. JOE VITALE

You want to become aware of your thoughts and choose your thoughts carefully and you want to have fun with this, because you are the masterpiece of your own life. You are the Michelangelo of your own life. The David you are sculpting is you.

One way to master your mind is to learn to quiet your mind. Without exception, every teacher in this book uses meditation as a daily practice. It wasn't until I discovered The Secret that I realized how powerful meditation can be. Meditation quiets your mind, helps you control your thoughts, and revitalizes your body. The great news is that you don't have to set aside hours to meditate. Just three to ten minutes a day to begin with, can be incredibly powerful for gaining control over your thoughts.

To become *aware* of your thoughts, you can also set the intention, "I am the master of my thoughts." Say it often, meditate on it, and as you hold to that intention, by the law of attraction you must become that.

You are now receiving the knowledge that will enable you to create the most magnificent version of You. The possibility of that version of you already exists on the frequency of "the most magnificent version of You." Decide what you want to be, do, and have, think the thoughts of it, emit the frequency, and your vision will become your life.

Secret Summaries

- *The Great Secret of Life is the law of attraction.*

- *The law of attraction says* like *attracts* like, *so when you think a thought, you are also attracting* like *thoughts to you.*

- *Thoughts are magnetic, and thoughts have a frequency. As you think thoughts, they are sent out into the Universe, and they magnetically attract all like things that are on the same frequency. Everything sent out returns to the source — you.*

- *You are like a human transmission tower, transmitting a frequency with your thoughts. If you want to change anything in your life, change the frequency by changing your thoughts.*

- *Your current thoughts are creating your future life. What you think about the most or focus on the most will appear as your life.*

- *Your thoughts become things.*

The Secret Made Simple

MICHAEL BERNARD BECKWITH

We live in a universe in which there are laws, just as there is a law of gravity. If you fall off a building it doesn't matter if you're a good person or a bad person, you're going to hit the ground.

The law of attraction is a law of nature. It is as impartial and impersonal as the law of gravity is. It is precise, and it is exact.

DR. JOE VITALE

Everything that surrounds you right now in your life, including the things you're complaining about, you've attracted. Now I know at first blush that's going to be something that you hate to hear. You're going to immediately say, "I didn't attract the car accident. I didn't attract this particular client who gives me a hard time. I didn't particularly attract the debt." And I'm here to be

27

a little bit in your face and to say, yes you did attract it.
This is one of the hardest concepts to get, but once you've
accepted it, it's life transforming.

Often when people first hear this part of the Secret they recall events in history where masses of lives were lost, and they find it incomprehensible that so many people could have attracted themselves to the event. By the law of attraction, they had to be on the same frequency as the event. It doesn't necessarily mean they thought of that exact event, but the frequency of their thoughts matched the frequency of the event. If people believe they can be in the wrong place at the wrong time, and they have no control over outside circumstances, those thoughts of fear, separation, and powerlessness, if persistent, can attract them to being in the wrong place at the wrong time.

You have a choice right now. Do you want to believe that it's just the luck of the draw and bad things can happen to you at any time? Do you want to believe that you can be in the wrong place at the wrong time? That you have no control over circumstances?

Or do you want to believe and *know* that your life experience is in your hands and that only all *good* can come into your life because that is the way you think? You have a choice, and whatever you choose to think *will* become your life experience.

Nothing can come into your experience unless you summon it through persistent thoughts.

BOB DOYLE

Most of us attract by default. We just think that we don't
have any control over it. Our thoughts and feelings are on
autopilot, and so everything is brought to us by default.

No one would ever deliberately attract anything unwanted. Without the knowledge of The Secret, it is easy to see how some unwanted things may have occurred in your life or other people's lives. It simply came from a lack of awareness of the great creative power of our thoughts.

DR. JOE VITALE

Now if this is your first time to hear this, it may feel like,
"Oh, I have to monitor my thoughts? This is going to be a lot
of work." It will seem like that at first, but that's where the
fun begins.

The fun is that there are many shortcuts to The Secret, and you get to choose the shortcuts that work best for you. Read on, and you'll see how.

MARCI SHIMOFF
AUTHOR, INTERNATIONAL SPEAKER, AND
TRANSFORMATIONAL LEADER

It's impossible to monitor every thought we have.
Researchers tell us that we have about sixty thousand
thoughts a day. Can you imagine how exhausted you'd

feel trying to control all sixty thousand of those thoughts?
Fortunately there's an easier way, and it's our feelings. Our
feelings let us know what we're thinking.

The importance of feelings cannot be overstated. Your feelings are your greatest tool to help you create your life. Your thoughts are the primary cause of everything. Everything else you see and experience in this world is effect, and that includes your feelings. The cause is always your thoughts.

Bob Doyle

The emotions are an incredible gift that we have to let us
know what we're thinking.

Your feelings tell you very quickly what you're thinking. Think about when your feelings suddenly took a dive—maybe when you heard some bad news. That feeling in your stomach or solar plexus was instant. So your feelings are an immediate signal for you to know what you are thinking.

You want to become *aware* of how you're feeling, and get in tune with how you're feeling, because it is the fastest way for you to know what you're thinking.

Lisa Nichols

You have two sets of feelings: good feelings and bad feelings.
And you know the difference between the two because one
makes you feel good, and the other makes you feel bad. It's the
depression, it's the anger, it's the resentment, it's the guilt. It's

those feelings that don't make you feel empowered. Those are
the bad feelings.

No one can tell you whether you are feeling good or bad, because you are the only one who knows how you're feeling at any time. If you're not sure how you're feeling, just ask yourself, "How am I feeling?" You can stop and ask this question often during the day, and as you do you will become more *aware* of how you're feeling.

The most important thing for you to know is that it is impossible to feel bad and at the same time be having good thoughts. That would defy the law, because your thoughts cause your feelings. If you are feeling bad, it is because you are thinking thoughts that are *making* you feel bad.

Your thoughts determine your frequency, and your feelings tell you immediately what frequency you are on. When you are feeling bad, you are on the frequency of drawing more bad things. The law of attraction *must* respond by broadcasting back to you more pictures of bad things and things that will make you feel bad.

As you feel bad, and don't make any effort to change your thoughts and feel better, you are in effect saying, "Bring me more circumstances that will make me feel bad. Bring it on!"

LISA NICHOLS

The flipside to that is that you have good emotions and good feelings. You know when they come because they make you feel good. Excitement, joy, gratitude, love. Imagine if we could

feel that way every day. When you celebrate the good feelings,
you'll draw to you more good feelings, and things that make
you feel good.

Bob Doyle

It's really so simple. "What am I attracting right now?" Well,
how do you feel? "I feel good." Well good, keep doing that.

It is impossible to feel good and at the same time be having negative thoughts. If you are feeling good, it is because you are thinking
good thoughts. You see, you can have whatever you want in your
life, no limits. But there's one catch: You have to feel good. And
when you think about it, isn't that all you ever want? The law is
indeed perfect.

Marci Shimoff

If you're feeling good, then you're creating a future that's on
track with your desires. If you're feeling bad, you're creating
a future that's off track with your desires. As you go about
your day, the law of attraction is working in every second.
Everything we think and feel is creating our future. If you're
worried or in fear, then you're bringing more of that into your
life throughout the day.

When you are feeling good, you must be thinking good thoughts.
So you are on track and you are emitting a powerful frequency that
is attracting back to you more good things that will make you feel
good. Seize those moments when you are feeling good, and milk

them. Be aware that as you are feeling good, you are powerfully attracting more good things to you.

Let's go one step further. What if your feelings are actually communication from the *Universe* to let you know what you're thinking?

JACK CANFIELD

Our feelings are a feedback mechanism to us about whether we're on track or not, whether we're on course or off course.

Remember that your thoughts are the primary cause of everything. So when you think a sustained thought it is immediately sent out into the Universe. That thought magnetically attaches itself to the *like* frequency, and then within seconds sends the reading of that frequency back to you through your feelings. Put another way, your feelings are communication back to you from the Universe, telling you what frequency you are currently on. *Your feelings are your frequency feedback mechanism!*

When you are feeling good feelings, it is communication back from the Universe saying, "You are thinking good thoughts." Likewise, when you are feeling bad, you are receiving communication back from the Universe saying, "You are thinking bad thoughts."

So when you are feeling bad it is communication from the Universe, and in effect it is saying, "Warning! Change thinking now. Negative frequency recording. Change frequency. Counting down to manifestation. Warning!"

The next time you are feeling bad or feeling any negative emotion, listen to the signal you are receiving from the Universe. In that moment you are *blocking* your own good from coming to you because you are on a negative frequency. Change your thoughts and think about something good, and when the good feelings start to come you will *know* it was because You shifted yourself on to a new frequency, and the Universe has confirmed it with better feelings.

BOB DOYLE

You're getting exactly what you're feeling about, not so much what you're thinking about.

That's why people tend to spiral if they stub their toe getting out of bed. Their whole day goes like that. They have no clue that a simple shifting of their emotions can change their entire day—and life.

If you start out having a good day and you're in that particular happy feeling, as long as you don't allow something to change your mood, you're going to continue to attract, by the law of attraction, more situations and people that sustain that happy feeling.

We all have experienced those days or times when one thing after another goes wrong. The chain reaction began with *one* thought, whether you were aware of it or not. The one bad thought attracted more bad thoughts, the frequency locked in, and eventually something went wrong. Then as you reacted to that one thing going wrong, you attracted more things going wrong. Reactions just attract more of the same, and the chain reaction must keep occurring until you move yourself off that frequency by intentionally changing your thoughts.

You can shift your thoughts to what you want, receive confirmation through your feelings that you changed your frequency, and the law of attraction will grab hold of that new frequency and send it back to you as the new pictures of your life.

Now here is where you can harness your feelings and use them to turbo-charge what you want in your life.

You can purposefully use your feelings to transmit an even more powerful frequency, by adding *feeling* to what you are wanting.

MICHAEL BERNARD BECKWITH

You can begin right now to feel healthy. You can begin to feel prosperous. You can begin to feel the love that's surrounding you, even if it's not there. And what will happen is the universe will correspond to the nature of your song. The universe will correspond to the nature of that inner feeling and manifest, because that's the way you feel.

So what are you feeling now? Take a few moments to think about how you feel. If you're not feeling as good as you'd like to, focus on *feeling* your feelings inside and purposefully lift them. As you focus intensely on your feelings, with the intention to lift yourself, you can powerfully elevate them. One way is to close your eyes (shutting out distractions), focus on your feelings inside, and smile for one minute.

LISA NICHOLS

Your thoughts and your feelings create your life. It will always be that way. Guaranteed!

Just like the law of gravity, the law of attraction never slips up. You don't see pigs flying because the law of gravity made a mistake and forgot to apply gravity to pigs that day. Likewise, there are no exclusions to the law of attraction. If something came to you, you drew it, with prolonged thought. The law of attraction is precise.

MICHAEL BERNARD BECKWITH

It's hard to swallow, but when we can begin to open ourselves up to that, the ramifications are awesome. It means that whatever thought has done in your life, it can be undone through a shift in your awareness.

You have the power to change anything, because you are the one who chooses your thoughts and you are the one who feels your feelings.

"You create your own universe as you go along."

Winston Churchill

DR. JOE VITALE

It's really important that you feel good, because this feeling good is what goes out as a signal into the Universe and starts to attract more of itself to you. So the more you can feel good, the more you will attract the things that help you feel good, and are able to keep bringing you up higher and higher.

BOB PROCTOR

When you're feeling down, did you know that you can change it in an instant? Put on a beautiful piece of music, or start singing—that'll change your emotion. Or think of something beautiful. Think of a baby or somebody that you truly love, and dwell on it. Really keep that thought in your mind. Block everything out but that thought. I guarantee you'll start to feel good.

Make a list of some Secret Shifters to have up your sleeve. By Secret Shifters, I mean things that can change your feelings in a snap. It might be beautiful memories, future events, funny moments, nature, a person you love, your favorite music. Then if you find yourself angry or frustrated or not feeling good, turn to your Secret Shifters list and focus on one of them. Different things will shift you at different times, so if one doesn't work, go to another. It only takes a minute or two of changing focus to shift yourself and shift your frequency.

Love: The Greatest Emotion

JAMES RAY
PHILOSOPHER, LECTURER, AUTHOR, AND CREATOR OF PROSPERITY AND HUMAN POTENTIAL PROGRAMS

The principle of feeling good applies to your family pets, for instance. Animals are wonderful, because they put you in a great emotional state. When you feel love for your pet, that great state of love will bring goodness into your life. And what a gift that is.

> "It is the combination of thought and love which forms the irresistible force of the law of attraction."
>
> *Charles Haanel*

There is no greater power in the Universe than the power of love. The feeling of love is the highest frequency you can emit. If you could wrap every thought in love, if you could love everything and everyone, your life would be transformed.

In fact, some of the great thinkers of the past referred to the law of attraction as the law of love. And if you think about it, you will understand why. If you think unkind thoughts about someone else, *you* will experience those unkind thoughts manifested. You cannot harm another with your thoughts, you only harm You. If you think thoughts of love, guess who receives the benefits—you! So if your predominant state is love, the law of attraction or the law of love responds with the mightiest force because you are on the highest frequency possible. The greater the love you feel and emit, the greater the power you are harnessing.

> "The principle which gives the thought the dynamic power to correlate with its object, and therefore to master every adverse human experience, is the law of attraction, which is another name for love. This is an eternal and fundamental principle inherent in all things, in every system of philosophy, in every Religion and in every Science. There is no getting away from the law of love. It is feeling that imparts vitality to thought. Feeling is desire and desire is love. Thought impregnated with love becomes invincible."
>
> *Charles Haanel*

MARCI SHIMOFF

Once you begin to understand and truly master your thoughts and feelings, that's when you see how you create your own reality. That's where your freedom is, that's where all your power is.

Marci Shimoff shared a wonderful quote from the great Albert Einstein: "The most important question any human being can ask themselves is, 'Is this a friendly Universe?'"

Knowing the law of attraction, the only answer to give is, "Yes, the Universe is friendly." Why? Because when you answer in this way, by the law of attraction you must experience that. Albert Einstein posed this powerful question because he knew The Secret. He knew by asking the question it would force us to think and make a choice. He gave us a great opportunity, just by posing the question.

To take Einstein's intention even further, you can affirm and proclaim, "This is a magnificent Universe. The Universe is bringing all good things to me. The Universe is conspiring for me in all things. The Universe is supporting me in everything I do. The Universe meets all my needs immediately." *Know* that this is a friendly Universe!

JACK CANFIELD

Since I learned The Secret and started applying it to my life, my life has truly become magical. I think the kind of life that everybody dreams of is one I live on a day-to-day basis. I live in a four-and-a-half-million-dollar mansion. I have a wife to die for. I get to vacation in all the fabulous spots of the world. I've climbed mountains. I've explored. I've been on safaris. And all of this happened, and continues to happen, because of knowing how to apply The Secret.

BOB PROCTOR

Life can be absolutely phenomenal, and it should be, and it will be, when you start using The Secret.

This is *your* life, and it's been waiting for you to discover it! Up until now you may have been thinking that life is hard and a struggle, and so by the law of attraction you will have experienced life as hard and a struggle. Begin right now to shout to the universe, "Life is so easy! Life is so good! All good things come to me!"

There is a truth deep down inside of you that has been waiting for you to discover it, and that Truth is this: *you deserve all good things life has to offer*. You know that inherently, because you feel awful when you are experiencing the lack of good things. All good things are your birthright! You are the creator of you, and the law of attraction is your magnificent tool to create whatever you want in your life. Welcome to the magic of life, and the magnificence of You!

Secret Summaries

- *The law of attraction is a law of nature. It is as impartial as the law of gravity.*

- *Nothing can come into your experience unless you summon it through persistent thoughts.*

- *To know what you're thinking, ask yourself how you are feeling. Emotions are valuable tools that instantly tell us what we are thinking.*

- *It is impossible to feel bad and at the same time have good thoughts.*

- *Your thoughts determine your frequency, and your feelings tell you immediately what frequency you are on. When you feel bad, you are on the frequency of drawing more bad things. When you feel good, you are powerfully attracting more good things to you.*

- *Secret Shifters, such as pleasant memories, nature, or your favorite music, can change your feelings and shift your frequency in an instant.*

- *The feeling of love is the highest frequency you can emit. The greater the love you feel and emit, the greater the power you are harnessing.*

How to Use The Secret

You are a creator, and there is an easy process to create using the law of attraction. The greatest teachers and avatars have shared the Creative Process through their wondrous work, in a myriad of forms. Some great teachers created stories to demonstrate how the Universe works. The wisdom contained in their stories has been handed down through the centuries and has become legendary. Many people living today do not realize that the essence of these stories is the very truth of life.

JAMES RAY

If you think about Aladdin and his lamp, Aladdin picks up the lamp, dusts it off, and out pops the Genie. The Genie always says one thing:

"Your wish is my command!"

The story now goes that there are three wishes, but if you trace the story back to its origins there's absolutely no limit whatsoever to the wishes.

Think about that one.

Now, let's take this metaphor and apply it to your life. Remember Aladdin is the one who always asks for what he wants. Then you've got the Universe at large, which is the Genie. Traditions have called it so many things—your holy guardian angel, your higher self. We can put any label on it, and you choose the one that works best for you, but every tradition has told us there's something bigger than us. And the Genie always says one thing:

"Your wish is my command!"

This wonderful story demonstrates how your whole life and everything in it has been created by You. The Genie has simply answered your every command. The Genie is the law of attraction, and it is always present and always listening to everything you think, speak, and act. The Genie assumes that everything you think about, you want! That everything you speak about, you want! That everything you act upon is what you want! You are the Master of the Universe, and the Genie is there to serve you. The Genie never questions your commands. You think it, and the Genie immediately begins to leverage the Universe, through people, circumstances, and events, to fulfill your wish.

The Creative Process

The Creative Process used in The Secret, which was taken from the New Testament in the Bible, is an easy guideline for you to create what you want in three simple steps.

Step 1: Ask

LISA NICHOLS

The first step is to ask. Make a command to the Universe. Let the Universe know what you want. The Universe responds to your thoughts.

BOB PROCTOR

What do you really want? Sit down and write it out on a piece of paper. Write it in the present tense. You might begin by writing, "I am so happy and grateful now that . . ." And then explain how you want your life to be, in every area.

You get to choose what you want, but you must get clear about what you want. This is your work. If you're not clear, then the law of attraction cannot bring you what you want. You will be sending out a mixed frequency and you can only attract mixed results. For the first time in your life perhaps, work out what it is you really want. Now that you know you can have, be, or do anything, and there are no limits, what do you want?

Asking is the first step in the Creative Process, so make it a habit to ask. If you have to make a choice and you don't know which way to go, ask! You should never be stumped on anything in your life. Just ask!

DR. JOE VITALE

This is really fun. It's like having the Universe as your catalogue. You flip through it and say, "I'd like to have this experience and I'd like to have that product and I'd like to have a person like that." It is You placing your order with the Universe. It's really that easy.

You do not have to ask over and over again. Just ask once. It is exactly like placing an order from a catalogue. You only ever order something once. You don't place an order and then doubt the order has been received and so place the order again, and then again, and then again. You order once. It is the same with the Creative Process. Step One is simply your step to get clear about what you want. As you get clear in your mind, you have asked.

Step 2: Believe

LISA NICHOLS

Step two is believe. Believe that it's already yours. Have what I love to call unwavering faith. Believing in the unseen.

You must believe that you have received. You must know that what you want is yours the moment you ask. You must have complete and utter faith. If you had placed an order from a catalogue you would relax, know you are going to receive what you ordered, and get on with your life.

> "See the things that you want as already yours.
> Know that they will come to you at need. Then
> let them come. Don't fret and worry about them.
> Don't think about your lack of them. Think of
> them as yours, as belonging to you, as already in
> your possession."

Robert Collier (1885–1950)

In the moment you ask, and *believe* and *know* you already have it in the unseen, the entire Universe shifts to bring it into the seen. You must act, speak, and think, as though you are receiving it *now*. Why? The Universe is a mirror, and the law of attraction is mirroring back to you your dominant thoughts. So doesn't it make sense that you have to see yourself as receiving it? If your thoughts contain noticing you do not have it yet, you will continue to attract not having it yet. You must believe you have it already. You must believe you have received it. You have to emit the feeling frequency of having received it, to bring those pictures back as your life. When you do that, the law of attraction will powerfully move all circumstances, people, and events, for you to receive.

When you book a vacation, order a brand new car, or buy a house, you know those things are yours. You wouldn't go and book another vacation for the same time, or purchase another car or house. If you won a lottery or received a large inheritance, even before you physically had the money, you know it is yours. That is the feeling of believing it is yours. That is the feeling of believing you have it already. That is the feeling of believing you have received. Claim the things you want by feeling and believing they are yours. When you do that, the law of attraction will powerfully move all circumstances, people, and events for you to receive.

How do you get yourself to a point of believing? Start make-believing. Be like a child, and make-believe. Act as if you have it already. As you make-believe, you will begin to *believe* you have received. The Genie is responding to your predominant thoughts all the time, not just in the moment you ask. That's why after you've asked, you must continue to *believe* and *know.* Have faith. Your belief that you have it, that undying faith, is your greatest power. When you believe you are receiving, get ready, and watch the magic begin!

> "You can have what you want—if you know
> how to form the mold for it in your own
> thoughts. There is no dream that may not come
> true, if you but learn to use the Creative Force
> working through you. The methods that work
> for one will work for all. The key to power lies in
> using what you have . . . freely, fully . . . and thus

opening wide your channels for more Creative
Force to flow through you."

Robert Collier

DR. JOE VITALE

*The Universe will start to rearrange itself to make it happen
for you.*

JACK CANFIELD

*Most of us have never allowed ourselves to want what we
truly want, because we can't see how it's going to manifest.*

BOB PROCTOR

*If you do just a little research, it is going to become evident
to you that anyone that ever accomplished anything, did not
know how they were going to do it. They only knew they were
going to do it.*

DR. JOE VITALE

*You don't need to know how it's going to come about. You
don't need to know how the Universe will rearrange itself.*

How it will happen, *how* the Universe will bring it to you, is not
your concern or job. Allow the Universe to do it for you. When
you are trying to work out *how* it will happen, you are emitting a
frequency that contains a lack of faith—that you don't believe you
have it already. You think *you* have to do it and you do not believe
the Universe will do it *for* you. The *how* is not your part in the
Creative Process.

BOB PROCTOR

You don't know how, it will be shown to you. You will attract the way.

LISA NICHOLS

Most of the time, when we don't see the things that we've requested, we get frustrated. We get disappointed. And we begin to become doubtful. The doubt brings about a feeling of disappointment. Take that doubt and shift it. Recognize that feeling and replace it with a feeling of unwavering faith. "I know that it's on its way."

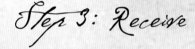

Step 3: Receive

LISA NICHOLS

Step three, and the final step in the process, is to receive. Begin to feel wonderful about it. Feel the way you will feel once it arrives. Feel it now.

MARCI SHIMOFF

And in this process it's important to feel good, to be happy, because when you're feeling good you're putting yourself in the frequency of what you want.

MICHAEL BERNARD BECKWITH

This is a feeling Universe. If you just intellectually believe something, but you have no corresponding feeling underneath

that, you don't necessarily have enough power to manifest
what you want in your life. You have to feel it.

Ask once, believe you have received, and all you have to do to receive is feel good. When you are feeling good, you are on the frequency of receiving. You are on the frequency of all good things coming to you, and you will receive what you have asked for. You wouldn't ask for anything unless it was going to make you feel good in the receiving of it, would you? So get yourself on the feel-good frequency, and you will receive.

A fast way to get yourself on that frequency is to say, "I am receiving now. I am receiving all the good in my life, now. I am receiving [fill in your desire] now." And *feel* it. *Feel* it as though you have received.

A dear friend of mine, Marcy, is one of the greatest manifestors I have seen, and she *feels* everything. She *feels* what it would feel like to have what she is asking for. She *feels* everything into existence. She doesn't get caught up in how, when, or where, she just *feels* it and it then manifests.

So *feel good* now.

BOB PROCTOR

When you turn that fantasy into a fact, you're in the position
to build bigger and bigger fantasies. And that, my friend, is
the Creative Process.

"Whatsoever ye shall ask in prayer, believing, ye shall receive."

Matthew 21:22

"What things soever ye desire, when ye pray, believe that ye receive them, and ye shall have them."

Mark 11:24

BOB DOYLE

The law of attraction, the study and practice of the law of attraction, is just figuring out what will help you generate the feelings of having it now. Go test drive that car. Go shop for that home. Get in the house. Do whatever you have to do to generate the feelings of having it now, and remember them. Whatever you can do to achieve that will help you to literally attract it.

When you *feel* as though you have it now, and the feeling is so real that it is like you have it already, you are believing that you have received, and you will receive.

BOB DOYLE

It could be you wake up and it's just there. It's manifested. Or, you might get some inspired idea of some action to take. You certainly shouldn't be saying, "Well, I could do it this way, but man, I would hate that." You're not on the right track if that's the case.

*Action will sometimes be required, but if you're really doing
it in line with what the Universe is trying to bring to you, it's
going to feel joyous. You're going to feel so alive. Time will
just stop. You could do it all day.*

Action is a word that can imply "work" to some people, but inspired action will not feel like work at all. The difference between
inspired action and action is this: Inspired action is when you are
acting to receive. If you are in action to try and make it happen,
you have slipped backward. Inspired action is effortless, and it
feels wonderful because you are on the frequency of receiving.

Imagine life as a fast-moving river. When you are acting to make
something happen it will feel as if you are going against the current
of the river. It will feel hard and like a struggle. When you are acting to receive from the Universe, you will feel as if you are flowing
with the current of the river. It will feel effortless. That is the feeling of inspired action, and of being in the flow of the Universe and
life.

Sometimes you will not even be aware you used "action" until
after you've received, because the acting felt so good. You will then
look back and see the wonder and matrix of how the Universe carried you to what you wanted, and also brought what you wanted
to you.

DR. JOE VITALE

*The Universe likes speed. Don't delay. Don't second guess.
Don't doubt. When the opportunity is there, when the impulse*

is there, when the intuitive nudge from within is there, act.
That's your job. And that's all you have to do.

Trust your instincts. It's the Universe inspiring you. It's the Universe communicating with you on the receiving frequency. If you have an intuitive or instinctive feeling, follow it, and you will find that the Universe is magnetically moving you to receive what you asked for.

BOB PROCTOR

You will attract everything that you require. If it's money you
need you will attract it. If it's people you need you'll attract
it. If it's a certain book you need you'll attract it. You've got
to pay attention to what you're attracted to, because as you
hold images of what you want, you're going to be attracted to
things and they're going to be attracted to you. But it literally
moves into physical reality with and through you. And it does
that by law.

Remember that you are a magnet, attracting everything to you. When you have gotten clear in your mind about what you want, you have become a magnet to draw those things to you, and those things you want are magnetized to you in return. The more you practice and begin to see the law of attraction bringing things to you, the greater the magnet you will become, because you will add the power of faith, belief, and knowing.

MICHAEL BERNARD BECKWITH

You can start with nothing, and out of nothing and out of no
way, a way will be made.

All you require is You, and your ability to think things into being. Everything that has been invented and created throughout the history of humankind began with one thought. From that one thought a way was made, and it manifested from the invisible into the visible.

JACK CANFIELD

Think of a car driving through the night. The headlights only go a hundred to two hundred feet forward, and you can make it all the way from California to New York driving through the dark, because all you have to see is the next two hundred feet. And that's how life tends to unfold before us. If we just trust that the next two hundred feet will unfold after that, and the next two hundred feet will unfold after that, your life will keep unfolding. And it will eventually get you to the destination of whatever it is you truly want, because you want it.

Trust the Universe. Trust and believe and have faith. I truly had no idea how I was going to bring the knowledge of The Secret onto the movie screen. I just held to the outcome of the vision, I saw the outcome clearly in my mind, I felt it with all my might, and everything that we needed to create *The Secret* came to us.

> "Take the first step in faith. You don't have to see the whole staircase. Just take the first step."
>
> Dr. *Martin Luther King, Jr.* (1929–1968)

The Secret and Your Body

Let's look at using the Creative Process for those who feel they are overweight and who want to lose weight.

The first thing to know is that if you focus on losing weight, you will attract back having to lose more weight, so get "having to lose weight" out of your mind. It's the very reason why diets don't work. Because you are focused on losing weight, you must attract back continually having to lose weight.

The second thing to know is that the condition of being overweight was created through your thought to it. To put it in the most basic terms, if someone is overweight, it came from thinking "fat thoughts," whether that person was aware of it or not. A person cannot think "thin thoughts" and be fat. It completely defies the law of attraction.

Whether people have been told they have a slow thyroid, a slow metabolism, or their body size is hereditary, these are all disguises for thinking "fat thoughts." If you accept any of those conditions as applicable to you, and you believe it, it must become your experience, and you will continue to attract being overweight.

After I had my two daughters I was overweight, and I know it came from listening to and reading the messages that it is hard to lose weight after having a baby, and even harder after the second baby. I summoned exactly that to me with those "fat thoughts," and it became my experience. I really "beefed up," and the more I noticed how I had "beefed up," the more "beefing up" I attracted. With a small frame, I became a hefty 143 pounds, all because I was thinking "fat thoughts."

The most common thought that people hold, and I held it too, is that food was responsible for my weight gain. That is a belief that does not serve you, and in my mind now it is complete balderdash! Food is not responsible for putting on weight. It is your *thought* that food is responsible for putting on weight that actually has food put on weight. Remember, thoughts are primary cause of everything, and the rest is effects from those thoughts. Think perfect thoughts and the result must be perfect weight.

Let go of all those limiting thoughts. Food cannot cause you to put on weight, unless you *think* it can.

The definition of the perfect weight is the weight that *feels* good for you. No one else's opinion counts. It is the weight that *feels* good for you.

You most likely know of someone who is thin and eats like a horse, and they proudly declare, "I can eat whatever I want and I am always the perfect weight." And so the Genie of the Universe says, "Your wish is my command!"

To attract your perfect weight and body using the Creative Process, follow these steps:

Step 1: Ask

Get clear on the weight you want to be. Have a picture in your mind of what you will look like when you have become that perfect weight. Get pictures of yourself at your perfect weight, if you have them, and look at them often. If not, get pictures of the body you would like to have and look at those often.

Step 2: Believe

You must believe you will receive and that the perfect weight is yours already. You must imagine, pretend, act as if, make-believe, that the perfect weight is yours. You must see yourself as receiving that perfect weight.

Write out your perfect weight and place it over the readout of your scale, or don't weigh yourself at all. Do not contradict what you have asked for with your thoughts, words, and actions. Don't buy clothes at your current weight. Have faith and focus on the clothes you are going to buy. Attracting the perfect weight is the same as placing an order with the catalogue of the Universe. You look through the catalogue, choose the perfect weight, place your order, and then it is delivered to you.

Make it your intention to look for, admire, and inwardly praise people with your idea of perfect-weight bodies. Seek them out and as you admire them and feel the feelings of that—you are summoning it to you. If you see people who are overweight, do not observe them, but immediately switch your mind to the picture of you in your perfect body and *feel* it.

Step 3: Receive

You must feel good. You must feel good about You. This is important, because you cannot attract your perfect weight if you feel bad about your body now. If you feel bad about your body, that is a powerful feeling, and you will continue to attract feeling bad about your body. You will never change your body if you are critical of it and find fault with it, and in fact you will attract more weight to you. Praise and bless every square inch of your body. Think about all the perfect things about You. As you think perfect thoughts, as you feel good about You, you are on the frequency of your perfect weight, and you are summoning perfection.

Wallace Wattles shares a wonderful tip about eating in one of his books. He recommends that when you eat, make sure you are entirely focused on the experience of chewing the food. Keep your mind present and experience the sensation of eating food, and do not allow your mind to drift to other things. Be present in your body and enjoy all the sensations of chewing the food in your mouth and swallowing it. Try it the next time you are eating. When you are completely present as you eat, the flavor of the food is so intense and magnificent; when you let your mind drift, the flavor virtually disappears. I am convinced that if we can eat our food in the present, entirely focused on the pleasurable experience of eating, the food is assimilated into our bodies perfectly, and the result in our bodies *must* be perfection.

The end of the story about my own weight is that I now maintain my perfect weight of 116 pounds and I can eat whatever I want. So, focus on your perfect weight!

How Long Does It Take?

DR. JOE VITALE

Another thing people wonder about is, "How long will it take to manifest the car, the relationship, the money?" I don't have any rulebook that says it's going to take thirty minutes or three days or thirty days. It's more a matter of you being in alignment with the Universe itself.

Time is just an illusion. Einstein told us that. If this is the first time you have heard it, you may find it a hard concept to get your head around, because you see everything happening—one thing after the other. What quantum physicists and Einstein tell us is that everything is happening simultaneously. If you can understand that there is no time, and accept that concept, then you will see that whatever you want in the future already exists. If everything is happening at the one time, then the parallel version of you with what you want *already* exists!

It takes no time for the Universe to manifest what you want. Any time delay you experience is due to your delay in getting to the place of believing, knowing, and feeling that you already have it. It is you getting yourself on the frequency of what you want. When you are on that frequency, then what you want will appear.

BOB DOYLE

Size is nothing to the Universe. It is no more difficult to attract, on a scientific level, something that we consider huge to something that we consider infinitesimally small.

The Universe does everything with zero effort. The grass doesn't strain to grow. It's effortless. It's just this great design.

It's all about what's going on in your mind. It's about what we put in place, saying, "This is big, it's going to take some time." And, "This is small. I'll give it an hour." Those are our rules that we define. There are no rules according to the Universe. You provide the feelings of having it now; it will respond—whatever it is.

There is no time for the Universe and there is no size for the Universe. It is as easy to manifest one dollar as it is to manifest one million dollars. It is the same process, and the only reason why one may come faster and the other may take longer is because you thought that a million dollars was a lot of money and that one dollar was not very much.

BOB DOYLE

Some people have an easier time with little things, and so we sometimes say start with something small, like a cup of coffee. Make it your intention to attract a cup of coffee today.

BOB PROCTOR

Hold an image of talking to an old friend that you haven't seen for a long time. Somehow or another somebody's going to start talking to you about that person. That person's going to phone you or you'll get a letter from her.

Starting with something small is an easy way to experience the law of attraction with your own eyes. Let me share a story with you of a young man who did exactly that. He watched *The Secret* and he decided to start with something small.

He created a picture of a feather in his mind, and he made sure this feather was unique. He created particular markings on the feather so he would know without any doubt that if he saw this feather, it had come to him through his intentional use of the law of attraction.

Two days later, he was about to walk into a high-rise building on a street in New York City. He said he did not know why, but he just happened to look down. There at his feet, at the entrance to a high-rise building in New York City, was the feather! Not just any feather, but the exact feather he had imagined. It was identical to the picture he had created in his mind, with all of its unique markings. In that moment he knew, without a shred of doubt, that this was the law of attraction working in all its glory. He realized his amazing ability and power to attract something to himself through the power of his mind. With total faith, he has now moved onto creating much bigger things.

DAVID SCHIRMER
INVESTMENT TRAINER, TEACHER, AND WEALTH SPECIALIST

People are amazed at how I line up parking spaces. I've done this right from when I first understood The Secret. I would visualize a parking space exactly where I wanted it, and 95 percent of the time it would be there for me and I would just pull straight in. Five percent of the time I'd have to wait just a minute or two, and the person would pull out and I'd pull in. I do that all the time.

Now you might understand why a person who says, "I always get parking spaces," gets them. Or why a person who says, "I am really lucky, I win things all the time," wins one thing after another, all the time. These people *expect* it. Begin to expect great things, and as you do, you will create your life in advance.

Create Your Day in Advance

You can use the law of attraction to create your whole life in advance, right down to the next thing you are doing today. Prentice Mulford, a teacher whose writings share so many insights into the law of attraction and how to use it, demonstrates how important it is to *think your day in advance*.

> "When you say to yourself, 'I am going to have a pleasant visit or a pleasant journey,' you are literally sending elements and forces ahead of your body that will arrange things to make your visit or journey pleasant. When before the visit or the journey or the shopping trip you are in a bad humor, or fearful or apprehensive of something unpleasant, you are sending unseen agencies ahead of you which will make some kind of unpleasantness. Our thoughts, or in other words, our state of mind, is ever at work 'fixing up' things good or bad in advance."

Prentice Mulford

Prentice Mulford wrote those words in the 1870s. What a pioneer! You can see clearly how important it is to *think in advance* every event in every day. You will no doubt have experienced the opposite of thinking your day in advance, and one of the repercussions of that is having to rush and hurry.

If you are rushing or hurrying, know that those thoughts and actions are based in fear (fear of being late) and you are "fixing up" bad things ahead for you. As you continue to rush, you will attract one bad thing after another into your path. In addition to that, the law of attraction is "fixing up" *more* future circumstances that will cause you to rush and hurry. You must *stop* and move yourself off that frequency. Take a few moments and shift yourself, if you don't want to summon bad things to you.

Many people, particularly in Western societies, chase "time" and complain that they *don't have enough time*. Well, as someone says that they don't have enough time, so it must be by the law of attraction. If you have been chasing your tail with thoughts of not having enough time, from now on declare emphatically, "I have more than enough time," and change your life.

You can also turn waiting into a powerful time to create your future life. Next time you are in a situation where you are waiting, seize that time and imagine having all the things you want. You can do this anywhere, anytime. Turn every life situation into a positive one!

Make it a daily habit to determine every event in your life in advance, through your thoughts. Set the Universal forces ahead of you in everything you do and everywhere you go, by thinking the way you want it to go *in advance*. Then you are creating your life intentionally.

Secret Summaries

- *Like Aladdin's Genie, the law of attraction grants our every command.*

- *The Creative Process helps you create what you want in three simple steps: ask, believe, and receive.*

- Asking *the Universe for what you want is your opportunity to get clear about what you want. As you get clear in your mind, you have asked.*

- Believing *involves acting, speaking, and thinking as though you have already received what you've asked for. When you emit the frequency of having received it, the law of attraction moves people, events, and circumstances for you to receive.*

- Receiving *involves feeling the way you will feel once your desire has manifested. Feeling good now puts you on the frequency of what you want.*

- *To lose weight, don't focus on "losing weight." Instead, focus on your perfect weight. Feel the feelings of your perfect weight, and you will summon it to you.*

- *It takes no time for the Universe to manifest what you want. It is as easy to manifest one dollar as it is to manifest one million dollars.*

- *Starting with something small, like a cup of coffee or parking spaces, is an easy way to experience the law of attraction in action. Powerfully intend to attract something small. As you experience the power you have to attract, you will move on to creating much bigger things.*

- *Create your day in advance by thinking the way you want it to go, and you will create your life intentionally.*

Powerful Processes

DR. JOE VITALE

A lot of people feel stuck or imprisoned or confined by their current circumstances. Whatever your circumstances right now, that is only your current reality, and current reality will begin to change as a result of beginning to use The Secret.

Your current reality or your current life is a result of the thoughts you have been thinking. All of that will totally change as you begin to change your thoughts and your feelings.

> "That a man can change himself . . . and master his
> own destiny is the conclusion of every mind who
> is wide-awake to the power of right thought."
>
> *Christian D. Larson* (1866–1954)

LISA NICHOLS

When you want to change your circumstances, you must first change your thinking. Every time you look inside your mail expecting to see a bill, guess what—it'll be there. Each day you go out dreading the bill! You're never expecting anything great. You're thinking debt, you're expecting debt. So debt must show up so you won't think you're crazy. And every day you confirm your thought: Is debt going to be there? Yes, debt's there. Is debt going to be there? Yes, debt's there. Is debt going to be there? Yes, debt's there. Why? Because you expected debt to be there. So it showed up, because the law of attraction is always being obedient to your thoughts. Do yourself a favor—expect a check!

Expectation is a powerful attractive force, because it draws things to you. As Bob Proctor says, "Desire connects you with the thing desired and expectation draws it into your life." Expect the things you want, and don't expect the things you don't want. What do you expect now?

JAMES RAY

Most people look at their current state of affairs and they say, "This is who I am." That's not who you are. That's who you were. *Let's say for instance that you don't have enough money in your bank account, or you don't have the relationship that you want, or your health and fitness aren't up to par. That's not who you are; that's the residual outcome of your past thoughts and actions. So we're constantly living in this residual, if you will, of the thoughts and actions we've taken in the past. When you look at your current state of affairs and define yourself by that, then you doom yourself to have nothing more than the same in future.*

"All that we are is a result of what we have thought."

Buddha (563 BCE–483 BCE)

I would like to share a process with you that came from the great teacher Neville Goddard in a lecture he delivered in 1954, entitled "The Pruning Shears of Revision." This process has had a profound effect on my life. Neville recommends at the end of every day, before you go to sleep, to think through the events of the day. If any events or moments did not go the way you wanted, replay them in your mind in a way that thrills you. As you recreate those events in your mind exactly as you want, you are cleaning up your frequency from the day and you are emitting a new signal and frequency for tomorrow. You have intentionally created new pictures for your future. It is never too late to change the pictures.

The Powerful Process of Gratitude

DR. JOE VITALE

What can you do right now to begin to turn your life around? The very first thing is to start making a list of things to be grateful for. This shifts your energy and starts to shift your thinking. Whereas before this exercise you might be focusing on what you don't have, your complaints, and your problems, you go in a different direction when you do this exercise. You start to be grateful for all the things that you feel good about.

> "If it is a new thought to you that gratitude
> brings your whole mind into closer harmony
> with the creative energies of the Universe,
> consider it well, and you will see that it is true."
>
> *Wallace Wattles* (1860–1911)

MARCI SHIMOFF

Gratitude is absolutely the way to bring more into your life.

DR. JOHN GRAY
PSYCHOLOGIST, AUTHOR, AND
INTERNATIONAL SPEAKER

Every man knows that when his wife is appreciating him for the little things that he does, what does he want to do? He wants to do more. It's always about appreciation. It pulls things in. It attracts support.

DR. JOHN DEMARTINI

Whatever we think about and thank about we bring about.

JAMES RAY

Gratitude has been such a powerful exercise for me. Every morning I get up and say "Thank you." Every morning, when my feet hit the floor, "Thank you." And then I start running through what I'm grateful for, as I'm brushing my teeth and doing the things I do in the morning. And I'm not just thinking about them and doing some rote routine. I'm putting it out there and I'm feeling the feelings of gratitude.

The day we filmed James Ray sharing his powerful exercise of gratitude is one I will never forget. From that day on, I made James's process my life. Every morning, I do not get out bed until I have felt the feelings of gratitude for this brand new day and all I am grateful for in my life. Then as I get out of bed, when one foot touches the ground I say, "Thank," and "you" as my second foot touches the ground. With each step I take on my way to the bathroom, I say "Thank you." I continue to say and feel "Thank you" as I am showering and getting ready. By the time I am ready for the day, I have said "Thank you" hundreds of times.

As I do this, I am powerfully creating my day and all that it will contain. I am setting my frequency for the day and intentionally declaring the way I want my day to go, rather than stumbling out of bed and letting the day take control of me. There is no more powerful way to begin your day than this. You are the creator of your life, and so begin by intentionally creating your day!

Gratitude was a fundamental part of the teachings of all the great avatars throughout history. In the book that changed my life, *The Science of Getting Rich*, written by Wallace Wattles in 1910, gratitude is its longest chapter. Every teacher featured in *The Secret* uses gratitude as part of his or her day. Most of them begin their day with thoughts and feelings of gratitude.

Joe Sugarman, a wonderful man and successful entrepreneur, watched the film *The Secret* and contacted me. He told me his favorite part was the gratitude process, and that his use of gratitude had contributed to all he had achieved in his life. With all the success Joe has attracted to himself, he continues to use gratitude every day, even for the smallest things. When he gets a parking space he always says and feels, "Thank you." Joe knows the power of gratitude and all it has brought to him, and so gratitude is his way of life.

With all that I have read and with all that I have experienced in my own life using The Secret, the power of gratitude stands above everything else. If you only do one thing with the knowledge of The Secret, use gratitude until it becomes your way of life.

DR. JOE VITALE

As soon as you start to feel different about what you already have, you will start to attract more of the good things. More of the things you can be grateful for. You could look around and say, "Well, I don't have the car I want. I don't have the house I want. I don't have the spouse I want. I don't have the health I want." Whoah! Back up, back up! Those are all the things you don't want. Focus on what you already have that you're grateful for. And it might be that you have the eyes to read this. It might be the clothes that you have. Yes, you might prefer something else and you might get something else pretty soon, if you start feeling grateful for what you have.

> "Many people who order their lives rightly in all other ways are kept in poverty by their lack of gratitude."
>
> *Wallace Wattles*

It is impossible to bring more into your life if you are feeling ungrateful about what you have. Why? Because the thoughts and feelings you emit as you feel ungrateful are all negative emotions. Whether it is jealousy, resentment, dissatisfaction, or feelings of "not enough," those feelings cannot bring you what you want.

They can only return to you more of what you do not want. Those negative emotions are blocking your own good coming to you. If you want a new car but you are not grateful for the car you have, that will be the dominant frequency you are sending out.

Be grateful for what you have now. As you begin to think about all the things in your life you are grateful for, you will be amazed at the never-ending thoughts that come back to you of more things to be grateful for. You have to make a start, and then the law of attraction will receive those grateful thoughts and give you more just like them. You will have locked into the frequency of gratitude and all good things will be yours.

> "The daily practice of gratitude is one of the conduits by which your wealth will come to you."
>
> *Wallace Wattles*

LEE BROWER
WEALTH TRAINER AND SPECIALIST, AUTHOR, AND TEACHER

I think everybody goes through times when they say, "Things aren't working right," or, "Things are going bad." Once, when there were some things going on in my family, I found a rock, and I just sat holding it. I took this rock, I stuck it in my pocket, and I said, "Every time I touch this rock I'm going to think of something that I'm grateful for." So every morning when I get up in the morning, I pick it up off the dresser, I put it in my pocket, and I go through the things that I'm grateful for. At night, what do I do? I empty my pocket, and there it is again.

I've had some amazing experiences with this idea. A guy from South Africa saw me drop it. He asked, "What is that?" I explained it to him, and he started calling it a gratitude rock. Two weeks later I got an email from him, in South Africa. And he said, "My son is dying from a rare disease. It's a type of hepatitis. Would you send me three gratitude rocks?" They were just ordinary rocks I found off the street, so I said, "Sure." I had to make sure that the rocks were very special, so I went out to the stream, picked out the right rocks, and sent them off to him.

Four or five months later I get an email from him. He said, "My son's better, he's doing terrific." And he said, "But you need to know something. We've sold over a thousand rocks at ten dollars apiece as gratitude rocks, and we've raised all this money for charity. Thank you very much."

So it's very important to have an "attitude of gratitude."

The great scientist Albert Einstein revolutionized the way we view time, space, and gravity. From his poor background and poor beginnings, you would have thought it impossible for him to achieve all that he did. Einstein knew a great deal of The Secret, and he said, "Thank you" hundreds of times each day. He thanked all the great scientists who had preceded him for their contributions, which had enabled him to learn and achieve even more in his work, and eventually become one of the greatest scientists who has ever lived.

One of the most powerful uses of gratitude can be incorporated in the Creative Process to turbo-charge what you want. As Bob Proctor advised in the first step of the Creative Process, *Ask*, start by writing down what you want. "Begin each sentence with, *I am so happy and grateful now that . . .*" (and you fill in the rest).

When you give thanks as though you have already received what you want, you are emitting a powerful signal to the Universe. That signal is saying that you have it already because you are feeling gratitude for it now. Each morning before you get out of bed, make it a habit to feel the feelings of gratitude *in advance* for the great day ahead, as though it is done.

From the moment I discovered The Secret and formulated the vision to share this knowledge with the world, I gave thanks every day for the film *The Secret*, which would bring joy to the world. I had no idea how we would bring this knowledge to the screen, but trusted that we would attract the way. I stayed focused and held to the outcome. I felt deep feelings of gratitude in advance. As that became my state of being, the floodgates opened and all the magic flowed into our lives. For the magnificent team of *The Secret*, and for me, our deep, heartfelt feelings of gratitude continue to this day. We have become a team that resonates gratitude with every moment, and it has become our way of life.

The Powerful Process of Visualization

Visualization is a process that has been taught by all the great teachers and avatars throughout the centuries, as well as by all the great teachers living today. In Charles Haanel's book, *The Master Key System*, written in 1912, he gives twenty-four weekly exercises to master visualization. (More important, his complete *Master Key System* will also help you become the master of your thoughts.)

The reason visualization is so powerful is because as you create pictures in your mind of seeing yourself with what it is you want, you are generating thoughts and feelings of having it now. Visualization is simply powerfully focused thought in pictures, and it causes equally powerful feelings. When you are visualizing, you are emitting that powerful frequency out into the Universe. The law of attraction will take hold of that powerful signal and return those pictures back to you, just as you saw them in your mind.

DR. DENIS WAITLEY

I took the visualization process from the Apollo program, and instituted it during the 1980s and '90s into the Olympic program. It was called Visual Motor Rehearsal.

When you visualize then you materialize. Here's an interesting thing about the mind: we took Olympic athletes

and had them run their event only in their mind, and then
hooked them up to sophisticated biofeedback equipment.
Incredibly, the same muscles fired in the same sequence when
they were running the race in their mind as when they were
running it on the track. How could this be? Because the mind
can't distinguish whether you're really doing it or whether it's
just a practice. If you've been there in the mind you'll go there
in the body.

Think about the inventors and their inventions: The Wright Brothers and the plane. George Eastman and film. Thomas Edison and the light bulb. Alexander Graham Bell and the telephone. The only way anything has ever been invented or created is because one person saw a picture in his mind. He saw it clearly, and by holding that picture of the end result in his mind, all the forces of the Universe brought his invention into the world, *through* him.

These men knew The Secret. These were men who had utter faith in the invisible, and who knew the power within them to leverage the Universe and bring the invention into the visible. Their faith and their imagination have been the cause of the evolution of humankind, and we reap the benefits of their creative minds every single day.

You may be thinking, "I do not have a mind like these great inventors." You may be thinking, "*They* could imagine those things, but I can't." You could not be further from the truth, and as you continue on this great discovery of the knowledge of The Secret, you will learn that you not only have the mind they had, but much more.

MIKE DOOLEY

When you're visualizing, when you've got that picture playing out in your mind, always and only dwell upon the end result.

Here's an example. Look at the back of your hands, right now. Really look at the back of your hands: the color of your skin, the freckles, the blood vessels, the rings, the fingernails. Take in all those details. Right before you close your eyes, see those hands, your fingers, wrapping around the steering wheel of your brand new car.

DR. JOE VITALE

This is such a holographic experience—so real in this moment—that you don't even feel as if you need the car, because it feels like you have it already.

Dr. Vitale's words brilliantly sum up the place you want to get yourself to when visualizing. When it feels like a jolt as you open your eyes in the physical world, your visualization became real. But that state, that plane, *is* the real. It is the field where everything is created, and the physical is just the *result* of the *real* field of all creation. That's why you won't feel as if you need it anymore, because you tuned in and felt the *real* field of creation through your visualization. In that field, you have everything now. When you feel that, you will know it.

JACK CANFIELD

It's the feeling that really creates the attraction, not just the picture or the thought. A lot of people think, "If I think positive thoughts, or if I visualize having what I want, that will be enough." But if you're doing that and still not feeling abundant, or feeling loving or joyful, then it doesn't create the power of the attraction.

BOB DOYLE

You put yourself in the feeling place of really being in that car. Not "I wish I could get that car," or, "Some day I'll have that car," because that's a very definite feeling associated with that. It's not in the now. It's in the future. If you stay in that feeling, it will always be in the future.

MICHAEL BERNARD BECKWITH

Now that feeling and that inner seeing will begin to be an open doorway through which the power of the Universe will begin to express.

"What this power is I cannot say. All I know is that it exists."

Alexander Graham Bell (1847–1922)

JACK CANFIELD

Our job is not to figure out the how. The how will show up out of a commitment and belief in the what.

MIKE DOOLEY

The "hows" are the domain of the Universe. It always knows the shortest, quickest, fastest, most harmonious way between you and your dream.

DR. JOE VITALE

If you turn it over to the Universe, you will be surprised and dazzled by what is delivered to you. This is where magic and miracles happen.

The teachers of The Secret are all aware of the elements you bring into play when you visualize. As you see the picture in your mind and feel it, you are bringing yourself to a place of believing you have it now. You are also implementing trust and faith in the Universe, because you are focusing on the end result and experiencing the feeling of that, without giving any attention whatsoever to "how" it will come about. Your picture in your mind is seeing it as done. Your feelings are seeing it as done. Your mind and your entire state of being are seeing it as *already happened*. That is the art of visualization.

DR. JOE VITALE

You want to do this virtually daily, but it should never be a chore. What's really important to the whole Secret is feeling good. You want to feel exhilarated by this whole process. You want to be high, happy, in tune, as much as possible.

Everyone has the power to visualize. Let me prove it to you with a picture of a kitchen. For this to work, first of all you have to get all thoughts of your kitchen out of your mind. Do *not* think of your kitchen. Totally clear your mind of pictures of your kitchen, with its cupboards, refrigerator, oven, tiles, and color scheme . . .

You saw a picture of your kitchen in your mind, didn't you? Well, then you just visualized!

> "Everyone visualizes whether he knows it or not. Visualizing is the great secret of success."
>
> *Genevieve Behrend* (1881–1960)

Here's a tip about visualizing, which Dr. John Demartini shares in his Breakthrough Experience seminars. John said that if you create a static picture in your mind it can be difficult to hold that picture, so create lots of movement in your picture.

To illustrate this, imagine your kitchen again, and this time imagine yourself entering that kitchen, walking to the refrigerator and putting your hand on the door handle, opening the door, looking inside, and finding a cold bottle of water. Reach in and grab it. You can feel the coldness on your hand as you grasp the bottle. You have the bottle of water in one hand, and you use your other hand to close the refrigerator door. Now that you are visualizing your kitchen with detail and movement it's easier to see and hold the picture, isn't it?

"We all possess more power and greater possibilities than we realize, and visualizing is one of the greatest of these powers."

Genevieve Behrend

The Powerful Processes in Action

MARCI SHIMOFF

The only difference between people who live in this way, who live in the magic of life, and those who don't is that the people who live in the magic of life have habituated ways of being. They've made a habit of using the law of attraction, and magic happens with them wherever they go. Because they remember to use it. They use it all the time, not just as a one-time event.

Here are two true stories that clearly demonstrate the powerful law of attraction and the immaculate matrix of the Universe in action.

The first story is about a woman named Jeannie, who bought a DVD of *The Secret* and was watching it at least once a day so that she would absorb the message right into the cells of her body. She was particularly impressed with Bob Proctor, and she thought it would be wonderful to meet him.

One morning Jeannie collected her mail, and to her utter amazement the mailman had accidentally delivered Bob Proctor's mail to her address. What Jeannie didn't know is that Bob Proctor lived just four blocks away from her! Not only that, but Jeannie's house number was the same number as Bob's. She immediately took the mail to deliver it to the correct address. Can you imagine her utter delight when the door opened and Bob Proctor was standing before her? Bob is rarely at home as he travels all over the world teaching, but the matrix of the Universe knows only perfect timing. From Jeannie's thought of how wonderful it would be to meet Bob Proctor, the law of attraction moved people, circumstances, and events throughout the Universe so that it happened.

The second story involves a ten-year-old boy named Colin, who had seen and loved *The Secret*. Colin's family made a weeklong visit to Disney World, and on their first day they experienced long lines at the park. So that night, just before Colin fell asleep, he thought, "Tomorrow I'd love to go on all the big rides and never have to wait in line."

The next morning, Colin and his family were at the gates of Epcot Center as the park opened, and a Disney staff member approached and asked them if they would be Epcot's First Family of the Day. As First Family they would be given VIP status, a special escort by a staff member, and walk-on passes for every big ride in Epcot. It was everything and more that Colin had wished for!

Hundreds of families were waiting to enter Epcot that morning, but Colin didn't have the slightest doubt as to why his family had been chosen First Family. He knew it was because he had used The Secret.

Imagine discovering—at the age of ten—that the power to move worlds lies within you!

> "Nothing can prevent your picture from coming into concrete form except the same power which gave it birth—yourself."
>
> *Genevieve Behrend*

JAMES RAY

People hold that for a while, and they're really a champion at it. They say, "I'm fired up. I saw this program and I'm going to change my life." And yet results aren't showing. Beneath the surface it's just about ready to break through, but the person will look just at the surface results and say, "This stuff doesn't work." And you know what? The Universe says, "Your wish is my command," and it disappears.

When you allow a thought of doubt to enter your mind, the law of attraction will soon line up one doubtful thought after another. The moment a thought of doubt comes, release it immediately. Send that thought on its way. Replace it with "I *know* I am receiving now." And feel it.

JOHN ASSARAF

Knowing the law of attraction, I wanted to really put it to use and to see what would happen. In 1995 I started to create something called a Vision Board, where I take something that

I want to achieve, or something that I want to attract, like a car or a watch or the soul mate of my dreams, and I put a picture of what I want up on this board. Every day I would sit in my office and I would look up at this board and I would start to visualize. I would really get into the state of having already acquired it.

I was getting ready to move. We put all the furniture, all the boxes, into storage, and I made three different moves over a period of five years. And then I ended up in California and bought this house, renovated it for a year, and then had all the stuff brought from my former home five years earlier. One morning my son Keenan came into my office, and one of the boxes that was sealed for five years was right at the doorstep. He asked, "What's in the boxes, Daddy?" And I said, "Those are my Vision Boards." He then asked, "What's a Vision Board?" I said, "Well, it's where I put all my goals up. I cut them out and I put all my goals up as something that I want to achieve in my life." Of course at five and a half years old he didn't understand, and so I said, "Sweetheart, let me just show you, that'll be the easiest way to do it."

I cut the box open, and on one Vision Board was a picture of a home that I was visualizing five years earlier. What was shocking was that we were living in that house. Not a house like it—I actually bought my dream home, renovated it, and didn't even know it. I looked at that house and I started to cry, because I was just blown away. Keenan asked, "Why are you crying?" "I finally understand how the law of attraction works. I finally understand the power of visualization. I finally understand everything that I've read, everything that I've worked with my whole life, the way I've built companies. It worked for my home as well, and I bought our dream home and didn't even know it."

"Imagination is everything. It is the preview of life's coming attractions."

Albert Einstein (1879–1955)

You can let your imagination go wild with a Vision Board, and place pictures of all the things you want, and pictures of how you want your life to be. Make sure you put the Vision Board in a place where you see it and look at it every day, as John Assaraf did. *Feel* the feelings of having those things now. As you receive, and feel gratitude for receiving, you can remove pictures and add new ones. This is a wonderful way to introduce children to the law of attraction. I hope the creation of a Vision Board inspires parents and teachers worldwide.

One of the people on The Secret website Forum put a picture of *The Secret* DVD on his Vision Board. He had seen *The Secret* but didn't own his own copy. Two days after he created his Vision Board, I felt inspired to post a notice on The Secret Forum giving away DVDs to the first ten people who posted. He was one of the ten! He had received a copy of *The Secret* DVD within two days of putting it on his Vision Board. Whether it is a DVD of *The Secret* or a house, the joy of creating and receiving is magnificent!

Another powerful example of visualizing comes from my mother's experience of buying a new house. Several people besides my mother had put in offers for this particular house. My mother decided to use The Secret to make that house hers. She sat down and wrote her name and the new address of the house over and over. She continued doing this until it felt as though it was her address. She then imagined placing all of her furniture in that new house. Within hours of doing these things, she received a phone call saying her offer had been accepted. She was so thrilled, but it didn't come as a surprise to her because she *knew* that house was hers. What a champion!

 ### JACK CANFIELD

Decide what you want. Believe you can have it. Believe you deserve it and believe it's possible for you. And then close your eyes every day for several minutes, and visualize having what you already want, feeling the feelings of already having it. Come out of that and focus on what you're grateful for already, and really enjoy it. Then go into your day and release it to the Universe and trust that the Universe will figure out how to manifest it.

Secret Summaries

- *Expectation is a powerful attractive force. Expect the things you want, and don't expect the things you don't want.*

- *Gratitude is a powerful process for shifting your energy and bringing more of what you want into your life. Be grateful for what you already have, and you will attract more good things.*

- *Giving thanks for what you want in advance turbo-charges your desires and sends a more powerful signal out into the Universe.*

- *Visualization is the process of creating pictures in your mind of yourself enjoying what you want. When you visualize, you generate powerful thoughts and feelings of having it now. The law of attraction then returns that reality to you, just as you saw it in your mind.*

- *To use the law of attraction to your advantage, make it a habitual way of being, not just a one-time event.*

- *At the end of every day, before you go to sleep, go back through the events of the day. Any events or moments that were not what you wanted, replay them in your mind the way you wanted them to go.*

The Secret to Money

"Whatever the mind . . . can conceive it can achieve."

W. Clement Stone (1902–2002)

JACK CANFIELD

The Secret was a real transformation for me, because I grew up with a very negative father who thought that rich people were people that had ripped everyone off and thought that anyone that had money must have deceived somebody. So I grew up with a lot of beliefs about money; that if you had it, it made you bad, only evil people have money, and money doesn't grow on trees. "Who do you think I am, Rockefeller?" That was one of his favorite phrases. So I grew up truly believing that life was difficult. It was only when I met W. Clement Stone that I began to shift my life.

When I was working with Stone he said, "I want you to set a goal that's so big that if you achieved it, it would blow your mind, and you would know it's only because of what I've taught you that you would have achieved this goal." At the time I was making about eight thousand dollars a year, so I said, "I want to make a hundred thousand dollars in a year." Now, I had no idea how I could do that. I saw no strategy, no possibility, but I just said, "I'm going to declare that, I'm going to believe it, I'm going to act as if it's true, and release it." So I did that.

One of the things he taught me was every day to close your eyes and visualize the goals as if it's already achieved. I had actually made a hundred-thousand-dollar bill that I'd put on the ceiling. So first thing in the morning I'd look up and there it was, and it would remind me that this was my intention. Then I would close my eyes and visualize having this hundred-thousand-dollar-a-year lifestyle. Interestingly enough, nothing major happened for about thirty days. I didn't have any great breakthrough ideas, no one was offering me more money.

About four weeks into it, I had a hundred-thousand-dollar idea. It just came right into my head. I had a book I had written, and I said, "If I can sell four hundred thousand copies of my book at a quarter each, that'd be a hundred thousand dollars." Now, the book was there, but I never had this thought. (One of The Secrets is that when you have an inspired thought, you have to trust it and act on it.) I didn't know how I was going to sell four hundred thousand copies.

Then I saw the National Enquirer *at the supermarket. I had seen that millions of times and it was just background. And all of a sudden it jumped out at me as foreground. I thought, "If readers knew about my book, certainly four hundred thousand people would go out and buy it."*

About six weeks later I gave a talk at Hunter College in New York to six hundred teachers, and afterward a woman approached me and said, "That was a great talk. I want to interview you. Let me give you my card." As it turns out, she was a freelance writer who sold her stories to the National Enquirer. *The theme from "The Twilight Zone" went off in my head, like, whoah, this stuff's really working. That article came out and our book sales started to take off.*

The point I want to make is that I was attracting into my life all these different events, including this person. To make a long story short, I did not make a hundred thousand dollars that year. We made ninety-two thousand three hundred and twenty-seven dollars. But do you think we were depressed and saying, "This doesn't work"? No, we were saying, "This is amazing!" So my wife said to me, "If it works for a hundred thousand, do you think it'd work for a million?" And I said, "I don't know, I think so. Let's try it."

My publisher wrote me a royalty check for our first Chicken Soup for the Soul *book. And he actually put a smiley face in his signature, because it was the first million-dollar check he'd ever written.*

So I know from my own experience, because I wanted to test it. Does this Secret really work? We put it to the test. It absolutely worked, and now I live my life from that every single day.

The knowledge of The Secret and the intentional use of the law of attraction can be applied to every single subject in your life. It is the same process for everything you want to create, and the subject of money is no different.

To attract money, you must focus on wealth. It is impossible to bring more money into your life when you are noticing you do not have enough, because that means you are thinking *thoughts* that you do not have enough. Focus on not enough money, and you will create untold more circumstances of not having enough money. You must focus on the abundance of money to bring that to you.

You have to emit a new signal with your thoughts, and those thoughts should be that you currently have more than enough. You really do need to call your imagination into play and make believe you already have the money you want. And it is so much fun to do! You will notice as you pretend and play games of having wealth that you feel instantly better about money, and as you feel better about it, it will begin to flow into your life.

Jack's wonderful story inspired The Secret Team to create a blank check available as a free download on The Secret website, www .thesecret.tv. The blank check is for you, and it is from the Bank of the Universe. You fill in your name, the amount, and details, and place it in a prominent place where you will see it every day. When you look at the check, feel the feelings of having that money now. Imagine spending that money, all the things you will buy and the things you will do. Feel how wonderful that is! Know it is yours, because when you ask, it is. We have received hundreds of stories from people who have brought huge sums of money to them using The Secret check. It's a fun game that works!

Attract Abundance

The only reason any person does not have enough money is because they are *blocking* money from coming to them with their thoughts. Every negative thought, feeling, or emotion is *blocking* your good from coming to you, and that includes money. It is not that the money is being kept from you by the Universe, because all the money you require exists right now in the invisible. If you do not have enough, it is because you are stopping the flow of money coming to you, and you are doing that with your thoughts. You must tip the balance of your thoughts from lack-of-money to more-than-enough-money. Think more thoughts of abundance than of lack, and you have tipped the balance.

When you *need* money, it is a powerful feeling within you, and so of course through the law of attraction you will continue to attract *needing* money.

I can speak from experience about money, because just before I discovered The Secret my accountants told me that my company had suffered a major loss that year, and in three months it would be history. After ten years of hard work, my company was about to slip through my fingers. And as I *needed* more money to save my company, things just got worse. There seemed no way out.

Then I discovered The Secret, and everything in my life—including the state of my company—was totally transformed, because I changed the way I was thinking. As my accountants continued to fuss about the figures and focus on that, I kept my mind focused on abundance and all being well. I *knew* with every fiber of my being that the Universe would provide, and it did. It provided in ways I could not have imagined. I had my moments of doubt, but when the doubt came I immediately moved my thoughts to the outcome of what I wanted. I gave thanks for it, I felt the joy of it, and I *believed*!

I want to let you in on a secret to The Secret. The shortcut to anything you want in your life is to BE and FEEL happy now! It is the fastest way to bring money and anything else you want into your life. Focus on radiating out into the Universe those feelings of joy and happiness. When you do that, you will attract back to you all things that bring you joy and happiness, which will not only include an abundance of money, but everything else you are wanting. You must radiate out the signal to bring back what you want. As you radiate out those feelings of happiness, they will be sent back to you as the pictures and experiences of your life. The law of attraction is reflecting back your innermost thoughts and feelings as your life.

Focus on Prosperity

 DR. JOE VITALE

*I can imagine what a lot of people are thinking: "How can I
attract more money into my life? How can I get more of the
green stuff? How can I get more of wealth and prosperity?
How can I, when I love my job, deal with the credit card debt
that I have, and the realization that maybe there's a ceiling on
the money that can come in, cause it's coming to me through
my job? How can I bring in more?" Intend it!*

*This goes back to one of the things we've been talking about
throughout the whole Secret. Your job is to declare what
you would like to have from the catalogue of the Universe. If
cash is one of them, say how much you would like to have. "I
would like to have twenty-five thousand dollars, unexpected
income, within the next thirty days," or whatever it happens
to be. It should be* believable *for you.*

If you have held thoughts in the past that the only way money can
come to you is through your job, then let that go immediately. Can
you appreciate that as you continue to think that, it *must* be your
experience? Such thoughts do not serve you.

You are now coming to understand that there is abundance for
you, and it is not your job to work out "how" the money will come
to you. It is your job to ask, to believe you are receiving, and feel

happy now. Leave the details to the Universe on how it will bring it about.

BOB PROCTOR

Most people have a goal of getting out of debt. That will keep you in debt forever. Whatever you're thinking about, you will attract. You say, "But it's get out of debt." I don't care if it's get out or get in, if you're thinking debt, you're attracting debt. Set up an automatic debt repayment program and then start to focus on prosperity.

When you have a pile of bills that you have no idea how you are going to pay, you cannot focus on those bills, because you will continue to attract more bills. You have to find a way that works for you to focus on prosperity, *despite* the bills around you. You have to find a way of feeling good, so you can bring your good to you.

JAMES RAY

So many times people say to me, "I'd like to double my income in the next year." But then you look at their actions and they're not doing the things that are going to make that happen. They'll turn right around and they'll say, "I can't afford that." Guess what? "Your wish is my command."

If the words "I can't afford it" have passed your lips, your power to change that is *now*. Change it with, "I can afford that! I can buy that!" Say it over and over. Become like a parrot. For the next thirty days, make it your intention that you are going to look at everything you like and say to yourself, "I can afford that. I can buy that." As you see your dream car drive past, say, "I can afford that." As you see clothes you love, as you think about a great vacation, say, "I can afford that." As you do this you will begin to shift yourself and you will begin to *feel* better about money. You will begin to convince yourself that you can afford those things, and as you do, the pictures of your life will change.

LISA NICHOLS

When you focus on lack and scarcity and what you don't have, you fuss about it with your family, you discuss it with your friends, you tell your children that you don't have enough—"We don't have enough for that, we can't afford that"—then you'll never be able to afford it, because you begin to attract more of what you don't have. If you want abundance, if you want prosperity, then focus on abundance. Focus on prosperity.

> "The spiritual substance from which comes all visible wealth is never depleted. It is right with you all the time and responds to your faith in it and your demands on it."
>
> *Charles Fillmore* (1854–1948)

Now that you know The Secret, when you see someone who is wealthy you will know that that person's predominant thoughts are on wealth and not on scarcity, and that they have *drawn* wealth to them—whether they did it consciously or unconsciously. They focused on thoughts of wealth and the Universe moved people, circumstances, and events to deliver wealth to them.

The wealth that they have, you have also. The only difference between you and them is that they thought the thoughts to bring the wealth to them. Your wealth is waiting for you in the invisible, and to bring it into the visible, think wealth!

DAVID SCHIRMER

When I first understood The Secret, every day I would get a bunch of bills in the mail. I thought, "How do I turn this around?" The law of attraction states that what you focus on you will get, so I got a bank statement, I whited out the total, and I put a new total in there. I put exactly how much I wanted to see in the bank. So I thought, "What if I just visualized checks coming in the mail?" So I just visualized a bunch of checks coming in the mail. Within just one month, things started to change. It is amazing; today I just get checks in the mail. I get a few bills, but I get more checks than bills.

Since the film *The Secret* was released, we have received hundreds and hundreds of letters from people who have said that since watching the film they have received unexpected checks in the mail. And it happened because as they gave their focus and attention to David's story, they brought checks to them.

A game I created that helped shift my feelings about my pile of bills was to pretend that the bills were actually checks. I would jump for joy as I opened them and say, "More money for me! Thank you. Thank you." I took each bill, imagined it was a check, and then I added a zero to it in my mind to make it even more. I got a notepad and wrote at the top of the page "I have received," and then I would list all the amounts of the bills with an added zero. Next to each amount I would write "Thank you," and feel the feelings of gratitude for receiving it—to the point where I had tears in my eyes. Then I would take each bill, which looked very small compared to what I had received, and I would pay it with gratitude!

I never opened my bills until I had got myself into the feeling that they were checks. If I opened my bills before convincing myself they were checks, my stomach would churn when I opened them. I knew that the emotion of the churning in my stomach was powerfully bringing more bills. I knew I had to erase that feeling, and replace it with joyful feelings, so I could bring more money into my life. In the face of a pile of bills, that game worked for me, and it changed my life. There are so many games you can create, and you will know what works best for you by the way you feel inside. When you make-believe, the results come fast!

LORAL LANGEMEIER

FINANCIAL STRATEGIST, SPEAKER, AND PERSONAL AND CORPORATE COACH

*I grew up on, "You have to work hard for money."
So I replaced that with, "Money comes easily and
frequently." Now in the beginning it feels like a lie, right?
There is a part of your brain that will say, "Oh you liar, it's
hard." So you have to know it's this little tennis match that
will go on for a while.*

If you have had thoughts of, "I have to work really hard and
struggle to have money," let them go immediately. By thinking
those thoughts you emitted that frequency, and they became the
pictures of your life experience. Take Loral Langemeier's advice,
and replace those thoughts with, "Money comes easily and frequently."

DAVID SCHIRMER

*When it comes to creating wealth, wealth is a mindset. It's all
about how you think.*

LORAL LANGEMEIER

*I'd say 80 percent of the coaching that I do with folks is
about their psychology and the way they think. I know
when people say, "Oh, you can do it, I can't." People
have the capability to change their inner relationship and
conversation with money.*

"The good news is that the moment you decide that what you know is more important than what you have been taught to believe, you will have shifted gears in your quest for abundance. Success comes from within, not from without."

Ralph Waldo Emerson (1803–1882)

You have got to *feel good* about money to attract more to you. Understandably, when people do not have enough money they do not feel good about money, because they don't have enough. But those negative feelings about money are stopping more money coming to you! You have got to stop the cycle, and you stop it by starting to feel good about money, and being grateful for what you have. Start to say and *feel*, "I have more than enough." "There is an abundance of money and it's on its way to me." "I am a money magnet." "I love money and money loves me." "I am receiving money every day." "Thank you. Thank you. Thank you."

Give Money to Get Money

Giving is a powerful action to bring more money into your life, because when you are giving you are saying, "I have plenty." It will not be surprising to you to learn that the wealthiest people on the planet are the greatest philanthropists. They give away vast amounts of money, and as they give, by the law of attraction, the Universe opens up and floods vast amounts of money back to them —multiplied!

If you are thinking, "I don't have enough money to give," bingo! Now you know why you don't have enough money! When you think you don't have enough to give, start giving. As you demonstrate faith in giving, the law of attraction must give you more to give.

There is a big difference between giving and sacrificing. Giving from a heart that is overflowing feels so good. Sacrificing does not feel good. Don't confuse the two—they are diametrically opposed. One emits a signal of lack and the other emits a signal of more-than-enough. One feels good and one does not feel good. Sacrifice will eventually lead to resentment. Giving from a full heart is one of the most joyous things you can do, and the law of attraction will grab hold of that signal and flood even more into your life. You can *feel* the difference.

JAMES RAY

I find so many people who make a tremendous amount of money, but their relationships stink. And that's not wealth. You can go after the money and you might get rich, but it doesn't guarantee you'll be wealthy. I'm not suggesting that money isn't a part of wealth, it absolutely is. But it's only a part.

*And then I meet a lot of people who are "spiritual," but
they're sick and broke all the time. That's not wealth either.
Life is meant to be abundant—in all areas.*

If you have been brought up to believe that being wealthy is not
spiritual, then I highly recommend you read The Millionaires of
the Bible Series by Catherine Ponder. In these glorious books you
will discover that Abraham, Isaac, Jacob, Joseph, Moses, and Jesus
were not only prosperity teachers, but also millionaires themselves, with more affluent lifestyles than many present-day millionaires could conceive of.

You are the heir to the kingdom. Prosperity is your birthright, and
you hold the key to more abundance—in every area of your life—
than you can possibly imagine. You deserve every good thing you
want, and the Universe will give you every good thing you want,
but you have to summon it into your life. Now you know The
Secret. You have the key. The key is your thoughts and feelings,
and you have been holding the key in your hand all of your life.

MARCI SHIMOFF

*Many people in Western culture are striving for success. They
want the great home, they want their businesses to work,
they want all these outer things. But what we found in our
research is that having these outer things does not necessarily
guarantee what we really want, which is happiness. So we
go for these outer things thinking they're going to bring us*

happiness, but it's backward. You need to go for the inner joy, the inner peace, the inner vision first, and then all of the outer things appear.

Everything you want is an inside job! The outside world is the world of effects; it's just the result of thoughts. Set your thoughts and frequency on happiness. Radiate the feelings of happiness and joy within you, and transmit that into the Universe with all of your might, and you will experience true heaven on earth.

Secret Summaries

- *To attract money, focus on wealth. It is impossible to bring more money into your life when you focus on the lack of it.*

- *It is helpful to use your imagination and make-believe you already have the money you want. Play games of having wealth and you will feel better about money; as you feel better about it, more will flow into your life.*

- *Feeling happy now is the fastest way to bring money into your life.*

- *Make it your intention to look at everything you like and say to yourself, "I can afford that. I can buy that." You will shift your thinking and begin to feel better about money.*

- *Give money in order to bring more of it into your life. When you are generous with money and feel good about sharing it, you are saying, "I have plenty."*

- *Visualize checks in the mail.*

- *Tip the balance of your thoughts to wealth. Think wealth.*

The Secret to Relationships

MARIE DIAMOND
FENG SHUI CONSULTANT, TEACHER, AND SPEAKER

The Secret means that we are creators of our Universe, and that every wish that we want to create will manifest in our lives. Therefore, our wishes, thoughts, and feelings are very important because they will manifest.

One day I went into the home of an art director, a very famous film producer. In every corner he had this beautiful image of a naked woman draped with a fabric, kind of turning away as if she were saying, "I don't see you." I said to him, "I think you might have trouble in your romance." And he said, "Are you clairvoyant?" "No, but look. In seven places, you have exactly that same woman." He said, "But I love that kind of painting. I painted it myself." I said, "That's even worse because you put all your creation and creativity in it."

He's a gorgeous-looking man with all these actresses around him because that's the work he does, and he doesn't have any romance. I asked him, "What do you want?" "I want to date three women a week." I said, "OK, paint it. Paint yourself with three women, and hang it in every corner of your living space."

Six months later I saw him and asked, "How is your love life?" "Great! Women call me, they want to date me." "Because that's your wish," I said. He said, "I feel great. I mean, for years I did not have a date and now I have three dates a week. They're fighting over me." "Good for you," I said. Then he told me, "I really want to stabilize. I want marriage now, I want romance." I said, "Well, then paint it." He painted a beautiful romantic relationship, and a year later he got married, and he's very happy.

This is because he put another wish out. He wished it in himself for years without it happening because his wish could not manifest. The outer level of himself—his house—was contradicting his wish all the time. So if you understand this knowledge, you just start playing with it.

Marie Diamond's story of her client is a perfect demonstration of how Feng Shui reflects the teachings of The Secret. It illustrates how our thoughts create powerfully when we put them into action. Any action we take must be preceded by a thought. Thoughts create the words we speak, the feelings we feel, and our actions. Actions are particularly powerful, because they are thoughts that have *caused* us to act.

We may not even realize what our innermost thoughts are, but we can see what we have been thinking by looking at the actions we have taken. In the story of the film producer, his innermost thoughts were reflected in his actions and surroundings. He had painted many women, all turning away from him. Can you see what his innermost thoughts were? Even though his words were saying he wanted to date more women, his innermost thoughts did not reflect that in his paintings. By deliberately choosing to change his actions, it caused him to focus his entire thought on what he wanted. With such a simple shift, he was able to paint his life and call it into existence through the law of attraction.

When you want to attract something into your life, make sure your actions don't contradict your desires. One of the most wonderful examples of this is given by Mike Dooley, one of the teachers featured in *The Secret*, in his audio course, *Leveraging the Universe and Engaging the Magic*. It is a story of a woman who wanted to attract her perfect partner into her life. She had done all the right things: She got clear about what she wanted him to be like, made a detailed list of all of his qualities, and visualized him in her life. Despite doing all these things, there was no sign of him.

Then one day as she arrived home and was parking her car in the middle of her garage, she gasped as she realized that her actions were contradicting what she wanted. If her car was in the middle of the garage, there was no room for her perfect partner's car! Her actions were powerfully saying to the Universe that she did not believe she was going to receive what she had asked for. So she immediately cleaned up her garage and parked her car to one side, leaving space for her perfect partner's car on the other side. She then went into her bedroom and opened her wardrobe, which was jammed full of clothes. There was no room for her perfect partner's clothes. So she moved some of her clothes to make space. She had also been sleeping in the middle of her bed, and so she began sleeping on "her" side, leaving space for her partner.

This woman related her story to Mike Dooley over a dinner, and sitting next to her at the table was her perfect partner. After taking all of these powerful actions and acting as if she had already received her perfect partner, he arrived in her life and they are now happily married.

Another simple example of "acting as if" is a story of my sister Glenda, who is the production manager of the film *The Secret*. She was living and working in Australia, and she wanted to move to the United States and work with me in our U.S. office. Glenda knew The Secret very well, and so she was doing all the right things to bring forth what she wanted, but months were passing by and she was still in Australia.

Glenda looked at her actions and realized she was not "acting as if" she was receiving what she had asked for. So she began to take powerful actions. She organized everything in her life for her departure. She canceled memberships, gave away things she would not need, and she got her suitcases out and packed them. Within four weeks, Glenda was in the United States working out of our U.S. office.

Think about what you have asked for, and make sure that your actions are mirroring what you expect to receive, and that they're not contradicting what you've asked for. Act as if you are receiving it. Do exactly what you would do if you were receiving it today, and take actions in your life to reflect that powerful expectation. Make room to receive your desires, and as you do, you are sending out that powerful signal of expectation.

Your Job Is You

LISA NICHOLS

Inside relationships it's important to first understand who's coming into the relationship, and not just your partner. You need to understand yourself first.

JAMES RAY

How can you ever expect anyone else to enjoy your company if you don't enjoy your own company? And so again, the law of attraction or The Secret is about bringing that into your life. You've got to get really, really clear. Here's the question I would ask you to consider: Do you treat yourself the way you want other people to treat you?

When you do not treat yourself the way you want others to treat you, you can never change the way things are. Your actions are your powerful thoughts, so if you do not treat yourself with love and respect, you are emitting a signal that is saying you are not important enough, worthy enough, or deserving. That signal will continue to be broadcast, and you will experience more situations of people not treating you well. The people are just the effect. Your thoughts are the cause. You must begin to treat yourself with love and respect, and emit that signal and get on that frequency. Then the law of attraction will move the entire Universe, and your life will be full of people who love and respect you.

Many people have sacrificed themselves for others, thinking when they sacrifice themselves they are being a good person. Wrong! To sacrifice yourself can only come from thoughts of absolute lack, because it is saying, "There is not enough for everyone, so I will go without." Those feelings do not feel good and will eventually lead to resentment. There is abundance for everybody and it is each person's responsibility to summon their own desires. You cannot summon for another person because you cannot think and feel for another. Your job is You. When you make feeling good a priority, that magnificent frequency will radiate and touch everyone close to you.

DR. JOHN GRAY

You become the solution for you. Don't point to another person and say, "Now you owe me and you need to give me more." Instead, give more to yourself. Take time off to give to yourself, and in a sense to fill yourself up to fullness, to where now you can overflow in giving.

"To acquire love . . . fill yourself up with it until
you become a magnet."

Charles Haanel

Many of us were taught to put ourselves last, and as a consequence
we attracted feelings of being unworthy and undeserving. As those
feelings lodged within us, we continued to attract more life situations that had us feel more unworthy and not enough. You must
change that thinking.

"Undoubtedly to some, the idea of giving so
much love to self will seem very cold, hard and
unmerciful. Still this matter may be seen in a
different light, when we find that 'looking out for
Number One,' as directed by the Infinite, is really
looking out for Number Two and is indeed the
only way to permanently benefit Number Two."

Prentice Mulford

Unless you fill yourself up first, you have nothing to give anybody.
Therefore it is imperative that you tend to You first. Attend to your
joy first. People are responsible for their own joy. When you tend
to your joy and do what makes you feel good, you are a joy to be
around and you are a shining example to every child and every
person in your life. When you are feeling joy you don't even have
to think about giving. It is a natural overflow.

LISA NICHOLS

I got into many relationships expecting my partner to show me my beauty, because I didn't see my own beauty. When I was growing up, my heroes or my "she-roes" were the Bionic Woman, Wonder Woman, and Charlie's Angels. And while they're wonderful, they didn't look like me. It wasn't until I fell in love with Lisa—I fell in love with my mocha skin, my full lips, my round hips, my curly black hair—it wasn't until that happened that the rest of the world was able to fall in love with me as well.

The reason you have to love You is because it is impossible to feel good if you don't love You. When you feel bad about yourself, you are blocking all the love and all the good that the Universe has for you.

When you feel bad about yourself it feels as though you are sucking the life out of you, because all of your good, on every single subject—including health, wealth, and love—is on the frequency of joy and feeling good. The feeling of having unlimited energy, and that amazing feeling of health and wellness, are all on the frequency of feeling good. When you don't feel good about You, you are on a frequency that is attracting more people, situations, and circumstances that will continue to make you feel bad about You.

You must change your focus and begin to think about all the things that are wonderful about You. Look for the positives in You. As you focus on those things, the law of attraction will show you more great things about You. You attract what you think about. All you have to do is begin with one prolonged thought of something good about You, and the law of attraction will respond by giving You more *like* thoughts. Look for the good things about You. Seek and ye shall find!

BOB PROCTOR

There's something so magnificent about you. I have been studying me for forty-four years. I wanna kiss myself sometimes! Because you're going to get to love yourself. I'm not talking about conceit. I'm talking about a healthy respect for yourself. And as you love yourself, you'll automatically love others.

MARCI SHIMOFF

In relationships we're so used to complaining about other people. For instance, "My coworkers are so lazy, my husband makes me so mad, my children are so difficult." It's always focusing on the other person. But for relationships to really work, we need to focus on what we appreciate about the other person, not what we're complaining about. When we're complaining about those things we're only getting more of those things.

Even if you're having a really hard time in a relationship—things aren't working, you're not getting along, someone's in your face—you still can turn that relationship around. Take a piece of paper, and for the next thirty days sit down and write all the things that you appreciate about that person. Think about all the reasons that you love them. You appreciate their sense of humor, you appreciate how supportive they are. And what you'll find is that when you focus on appreciating and acknowledging their strengths, that's what you'll get more of, and the problems will fade away.

LISA NICHOLS

Oftentimes you give others the opportunity to create your happiness, and many times they fail to create it the way you want it. Why? Because only one person can be in charge of your joy, of your bliss, and that's you. So even your parent, your child, your spouse—they do not have the control to create your happiness. They simply have the opportunity to share in your happiness. Your joy lies within you.

All your joy is on the frequency of love—the highest and the most powerful frequency of all. You can't hold love in your hand. You can only *feel* it in your heart. It is a state of being. You can see evidence of love being expressed through people, but love is a feeling, and you are the only one that can radiate and emit that feeling of love. Your ability to generate feelings of love is unlimited, and when you love you are in complete and utter harmony with the Universe. Love everything you can. Love everyone you can. Focus only on things you love, feel love, and you will experience that love and joy coming back to you—multiplied! The law of attraction must send you back more things to love. As you radiate love, it will appear as though the entire Universe is doing everything for you, moving every joyful thing to you, and moving every good person to you. In truth, it is.

Secret Summaries

- *When you want to attract a relationship, make sure your thoughts, words, actions, and surroundings don't contradict your desires.*

- *Your job is you. Unless you fill yourself up first, you have nothing to give anybody.*

- *Treat yourself with love and respect, and you will attract people who show you love and respect.*

- *When you feel bad about yourself, you block the love and instead you attract more people and situations that will continue to make you feel bad about you.*

- *Focus on the qualities you love about yourself and the law of attraction will show you more great things about you.*

- *To make a relationship work, focus on what you appreciate about the other person, and not your complaints. When you focus on the strengths, you will get more of them.*

The Secret to Health

DR. JOHN HAGELIN
QUANTUM PHYSICIST AND PUBLIC POLICY EXPERT

Our body is really the product of our thoughts. We're beginning to understand in medical science the degree to which the nature of thoughts and emotions actually determines the physical substance and structure and function of our bodies.

DR. JOHN DEMARTINI

We've known in the healing arts of a placebo effect. A placebo is something that supposedly has no impact and no effect on the body, like a sugar pill.

You tell the patient that this is just as effective, and what happens is the placebo sometimes has the same effect, if not greater effect, than the medication that is supposed to be

125

*designed for that effect. They have found out that the human
mind is the biggest factor in the healing arts, sometimes more
so than the medication.*

As you are becoming aware of the magnitude of The Secret, you
will begin to see more clearly the underlying truth of certain occurrences in humankind, including in the area of health. The placebo
effect is a powerful phenomenon. When patients *think* and truly
believe the tablet is a cure, they will *receive* what they *believe*, and
they will be cured.

DR. JOHN DEMARTINI

*If somebody is in a situation where they're sick and they have
an alternative to try to explore what is in their mind creating
it, versus using medicine, if it's an acute situation that could
really bring death to them, then obviously the medicine is a
wise thing to do, while they explore what the mind is about.
So you don't want to negate medicine. Every form of healing
has a place.*

Healing through the mind can work harmoniously with medicine. If
pain is involved, then medicine can help to eliminate that pain, which
then allows the person to be able to focus with great force on health.
"Thinking perfect health" is something anybody can do privately
within themselves, no matter what is happening around them.

LISA NICHOLS

*The Universe is a masterpiece of abundance. When you
open yourself to feel the abundance of the Universe, you'll*

*experience the wonder, joy, bliss, and all the great things that
the Universe has for you—good health, good wealth, good
nature. But when you shut yourself off with negative thoughts,
you'll feel the discomfort, you'll feel the aches, you'll feel the
pain, and you'll feel as if every day is painful to get through.*

DR. BEN JOHNSON
PHYSICIAN, AUTHOR, AND
LEADER IN ENERGY HEALING

*We've got a thousand different diagnoses and diseases
out there. They're just the weak link. They're all the result of
one thing: stress. If you put enough stress on the chain and
you put enough stress on the system, then one of the links
breaks.*

All stress begins with one negative thought. One thought that went
unchecked, and then more thoughts came and more, until stress
manifested. The effect is stress, but the cause was negative thinking, and it all began with one little negative thought. No matter
what you might have manifested, you can change it . . . with one
small positive thought and then another.

DR. JOHN DEMARTINI

*Our physiology creates disease to give us feedback, to let us
know we have an imbalanced perspective, or we're not being
loving and grateful. So the body's signs and symptoms are not
something terrible.*

Dr. Demartini is telling us that love and gratitude will dissolve all negativity in our lives, no matter what form it has taken. Love and gratitude can part seas, move mountains, and create miracles. And love and gratitude can dissolve any disease.

MICHAEL BERNARD BECKWITH

The question frequently asked is, "When a person has manifested a disease in the body temple or some kind of discomfort in their life, can it be turned around through the power of 'right' thinking?" And the answer is absolutely, yes.

Laughter Is the Best Medicine

CATHY GOODMAN, A PERSONAL STORY

I was diagnosed with breast cancer. I truly believed in my heart, with my strong faith, that I was already healed. Each day I would say, "Thank you for my healing." On and on and on I went, "Thank you for my healing." I believed in my heart I was healed. I saw myself as if cancer was never in my body.

One of the things I did to heal myself was to watch very funny movies. That's all we would do was just laugh, laugh, and laugh. We couldn't afford to put any stress in my life, because we knew stress was one of the worst things you can do while you're trying to heal yourself.

*From the time I was diagnosed to the time I was healed
was approximately three months. And that's without any
radiation or chemotherapy.*

This beautiful and inspiring story from Cathy Goodman demonstrates three magnificent powers in operation: The power of gratitude to heal, the power of faith to receive, and the power of laughter and joy to dissolve disease in our bodies.

Cathy was inspired to include laughter as part of her healing, after hearing about the story of Norman Cousins.

Norman had been diagnosed with an "incurable" disease. The doctors told him he had just a few months to live. Norman decided to heal himself. For three months all he did was watch funny movies and laugh, laugh, laugh. The disease left his body in those three months, and the doctors proclaimed his recovery a miracle.

As he laughed, Norman released all negativity, and he released the disease. Laughter really *is* the best medicine.

DR. BEN JOHNSON

We all come with a built-in basic program. It's called "self-healing." You get a wound, it grows back together. You get a bacterial infection, the immune system comes and takes care of those bacteria, and heals it up. The immune system is made to heal itself.

BOB PROCTOR

Disease cannot live in a body that's in a healthy emotional state. Your body is casting off millions of cells every second, and it's also creating millions of new cells at the same time.

DR. JOHN HAGELIN

In fact, parts of our body are literally replaced every day. Other parts take a few months, other parts a couple of years. But within a few years we each have a brand new physical body.

If our entire bodies are replaced within a few years, as science has proven, then how can it be that degeneration or illness remains in our bodies for years? It can only be held there by thought, by observation of the illness, and by the attention given to the illness.

Think Thoughts of Perfection

Think thoughts of perfection. Illness cannot exist in a body that has harmonious thoughts. Know there is only perfection, and as you observe perfection you must summon that to you. Imperfect thoughts are the cause of all humanity's ills, including disease, poverty, and unhappiness. When we think negative thoughts we are cutting ourselves off from our rightful heritage. Declare and intend, "I think perfect thoughts. I see only perfection. I am perfection."

I banished every bit of stiffness and lack of agility right out of my body. I focused on seeing my body as flexible and as perfect as a child's, and every stiff and aching joint vanished. I literally did this overnight.

You can see that beliefs about aging are all in our minds. Science explains that we have a brand new body in a very short time. Aging is limited thinking, so release those thoughts from your consciousness and know that your body is only months old, no matter how many birthdays you have chalked up in your mind. For your next birthday, do yourself a favor and celebrate it as your first birthday! Don't cover your cake with sixty candles, unless you want to summon aging to you. Unfortunately, Western society has become fixated on age, and in reality there is no such thing.

You can *think* your way to the perfect state of health, the perfect body, the perfect weight, and eternal youth. You can bring it into being, through your consistent thinking of perfection.

 ## BOB PROCTOR

If you have a disease, and you're focusing on it, and you're talking to people about it, you're going to create more diseased cells. See yourself living in a perfectly healthy body. Let the doctor look after the disease.

One of the things that people often do when they have an illness is talk about it all the time. That's because they're thinking about it all the time, so they're just verbalizing their thoughts. If you are feeling a little unwell, don't talk about it—unless you want more of it. Know that your thought was responsible and repeat as often as you can, "I feel wonderful. I feel so good," and really feel it. If you are not feeling great and somebody asks you how you are feeling, just be grateful that that person has reminded you to think thoughts of feeling well. Speak only the words of what you want.

You cannot "catch" anything unless you think you can, and think-ing you can is inviting it to you with your thought. You are also inviting illness if you are listening to people talking about their illness. As you listen you are giving all of your thought and focus to illness, and when you give all of your thought to something, you are asking for it. And you are certainly not helping them. You are adding energy to their illness. If you really want to help that person, change the conversation to good things, if you can, or be on your way. As you walk away, give your powerful thoughts and feelings to seeing that person well, and then let it go.

LISA NICHOLS

Let's say you have two people, both stricken with something, but one chooses to focus on joy. One chooses to live in possibility and hopefulness, focusing on all the reasons why she should be joyful and grateful. Then you have the second person. Same diagnosis, but the second chooses to focus on the disease, the pain, and the "woe is me."

BOB DOYLE

When people are completely focused on what's wrong and their symptoms, they will perpetuate it. The healing will not occur until they shift their attention from being sick to being well. Because that's the law of attraction.

> "Let us remember, so far as we can, that every unpleasant thought is a bad thing literally put in the body."
>
> *Prentice Mulford*

DR. JOHN HAGELIN

Happier thoughts lead to essentially a happier biochemistry. A happier, healthier body. Negative thoughts and stress have been shown to seriously degrade the body and the functioning of the brain, because it's our thoughts and emotions that are continuously reassembling, reorganizing, re-creating our body.

No matter what you have manifested in regards to your body, you can change it—inside and out. Start thinking happy thoughts and start *being* happy. Happiness is a *feeling* state of being. You have your finger on the "feeling happy" button. Press it now and keep your finger pressed down on it firmly, no matter what is happening around you.

DR. BEN JOHNSON

Remove physiological stress from the body, and the body does what it was designed to do. It heals itself.

You don't have to fight to get rid of a disease. Just the simple process of letting go of negative thoughts will allow your natural state of health to emerge within you. And your body will heal itself.

 ## MICHAEL BERNARD BECKWITH

I've seen kidneys regenerated. I've seen cancer dissolved. I've seen eyesight improve and come back.

I had been wearing reading glasses for about three years before I discovered The Secret. One night as I was tracing the knowledge of The Secret back through the centuries, I found myself reaching for my glasses to see what I was reading. And I stopped in my tracks. The realization of what I had done struck me like a lightning bolt.

I had listened to society's message that eyesight diminishes with age. I had watched people stretch their arms out so that they could read something. I had given my thought to eyesight diminishing with age, and I had brought it to me. I hadn't done it deliberately, but *I* had done it. I knew that what I had brought into being with thoughts I could change, so I immediately imagined myself seeing as clearly as when I was twenty-one years old. I saw myself in dark restaurants, on planes, and at my computer, reading clearly and effortlessly. And I said over and over, "I can see clearly, I can see clearly." I felt the feelings of gratitude and excitement for having clear vision. In three days my eyesight had been restored, and I now do not own reading glasses. *I can see clearly.*

When I told Dr. Ben Johnson, one of the teachers from *The Secret*, about what I had done, he said to me, "Do you realize what had to happen to your eyes for you to do that in three days?" I replied, "No, and thank goodness I didn't know, so that thought was not in my head! I just knew I could do it, and that I could do it fast." (Sometimes less information is better!)

Dr. Johnson eliminated an "incurable" disease from his own body, so the restoration of my eyesight seemed like nothing to me, compared with his own miracle story. In fact, I expected my eyesight to come back overnight, so three days was no miracle in my mind. Remember, time and size do not exist in the Universe. It is as easy to heal a pimple as a disease. The process is identical; the difference is in our minds. So if you have attracted some affliction to you, reduce it in your mind to the size of a pimple, let go of all negative thoughts, and then focus on the perfection of health.

Nothing Is Incurable

DR. JOHN DEMARTINI
I always say that incurable means "curable from within."

I believe and know that nothing is incurable. At some point in time, every so-called incurable disease has been cured. In my mind, and in the world I create, "incurable" does not exist. There is plenty of room for you in this world, so come join me and all who are here. It is the world where "miracles" are everyday occurrences. It is a world overflowing with total abundance, where *all* good things exist now, within you. Sounds like heaven, doesn't it? It is.

MICHAEL BERNARD BECKWITH

You can change your life and you can heal yourself.

MORRIS GOODMAN
AUTHOR AND INTERNATIONAL SPEAKER

My story begins on March 10, 1981. This day really changed my whole life. It was a day I'll never forget. I crashed an airplane. I ended up in the hospital completely paralyzed. My spinal cord was crushed, I broke the first and second cervical vertebrae, my swallowing reflex was destroyed, I couldn't eat or drink, my diaphragm was destroyed, I couldn't breathe. All I could do was blink my eyes. The doctors, of course, said I'd be a vegetable the rest of my life. All I'd be able to do is blink my eyes. That's the picture they saw of me, but it didn't matter what they thought. The main thing was what I thought. I pictured myself being a normal person again, walking out of that hospital.

The only thing I had to work with in the hospital was my mind, and once you have your mind, you can put things back together again.

I was hooked to a respirator and they said I'd never breathe on my own again because my diaphragm was destroyed. But a little voice kept saying to me, "Breathe deeply, breathe deeply." And finally I was weaned from it. They were at a loss for an explanation. I could not afford to allow anything

*to come into my mind that would distract me from my goal or
from my vision.*

*I had set a goal to walk out of the hospital on Christmas.
And I did. I walked out of the hospital on my own two feet.
They said it couldn't be done. That's a day I will never
forget.*

*For people who are sitting out there right now and are hurting, if I
wanted to sum up my life and sum up for people what they can do in
life, I would sum it up in six words: "Man becomes what he thinks
about."*

Morris Goodman is known as The Miracle Man. His story was
chosen for *The Secret* because it demonstrates the unfathomable
power and unlimited potential of the human mind. Morris knew
the power within him to bring about what he chose to think
about. Everything is possible. Morris Goodman's story has inspired thousands of people to think, imagine, and *feel* their way
back to health. He turned the greatest challenge of his life into the
greatest gift.

Since the film *The Secret* was released, we have been inundated
with miracle stories of all types of diseases dissolving from people's bodies after they watched *The Secret*. All things are possible
when you believe.

On the subject of health I would like to leave you with these illu-
minating words from Dr. Ben Johnson: "We are now entering the

era of energy medicine. Everything in the Universe has a frequency and all you have to do to is change a frequency or create an opposite frequency. That's how easy it is to change anything in the world, whether that's disease or emotional issues or whatever that is. This is huge. This is the biggest thing that we have ever come across."

Secret Summaries

- *The placebo effect is an example of the law of attraction in action. When a patient truly believes the tablet is a cure, he receives what he believes and is cured.*

- *"Focusing on perfect health" is something we can all do within ourselves, despite what may be happening on the outside.*

- *Laughter attracts joy, releases negativity, and leads to miraculous cures.*

- *Disease is held in the body by thought, by observation of the illness, and by the attention given to the illness. If you are feeling a little unwell, don't talk about it—unless you want more of it. If you listen to people talk about their illness, you add energy to their illness. Instead, change the conversation to good things, and give powerful thoughts to seeing those people in health.*

- *Beliefs about aging are all in our minds, so release those thoughts from your consciousness. Focus on health and eternal youth.*

- *Do not listen to society's messages about diseases and aging. Negative messages do not serve you.*

The Secret to the World

LISA NICHOLS

People have a tendency to look at the things that they want and say, "Yes, I like that, I want that." However, they look at the things that they don't want and they give them just as much energy, if not more, with the idea that they can stamp it out, they can eliminate it, obliterate it. In our society, we've become content with fighting against things. Fighting against cancer, fighting against poverty, fighting against war, fighting against drugs, fighting against terrorism, fighting against violence. We tend to fight everything we don't want, which actually creates more of a fight.

HALE DWOSKIN

TEACHER AND AUTHOR OF *THE SEDONA METHOD*

Anything we focus on we do create. So if we're really angry, for instance, at a war that's going on, or strife, or suffering, we're adding our energy to it. We're pushing ourselves, and that only creates resistance.

"What you resist persists."

Carl Jung (1875–1961)

BOB DOYLE

The reason that what you resist persists is because if you're resisting something, you're saying, "No, I don't want this thing, because it makes me feel this way—the way I am feeling right now." So you're putting out a really strong emotion of, "I really don't like this feeling," and then it comes racing toward you.

Resistance to anything is like trying to change the outside pictures after they have been transmitted. It's a futile pursuit. You have to go within and emit a new signal with your thoughts and feelings to create the new pictures.

As you resist what has appeared, you are adding more energy and more power to those pictures you don't like, and you are bringing more of them at a furious rate. The event or circumstances can only get bigger, because that is the law of the Universe.

JACK CANFIELD

The anti-war movement creates more war. The anti-drug movement has actually created more drugs. Because we're focusing on what we don't want—drugs!

LISA NICHOLS

*People believe that if we really want to eliminate something,
focus on that. How much sense does it make for us to give
the particular problem all of the energy, as opposed to
focusing on trust, love, living in abundance, education, or
peace?*

JACK CANFIELD

*Mother Teresa was brilliant. She said, "I will never attend an
anti-war rally. If you have a peace rally, invite me." She knew.
She understood The Secret. Look what she manifested in the
world.*

HALE DWOSKIN

*So if you're anti-war, be pro-peace instead. If you're anti-
hunger, be pro-people having more than enough to eat. If you
are anti-a-particular politician, be pro-his opponent. Often
elections are tipped in favor of the person that the people are
really against, because he's getting all the energy and all the
focus.*

Everything in this world began with one thought. The bigger things
get bigger because more people give their thoughts to it after it has
appeared. Then those thoughts and emotions keep that very event
in our existence, and make it bigger. If we took our minds off it and
focused instead on love, it could not exist. It would evaporate and
disappear.

"Remember, and this is one of the most difficult
as well as most wonderful statements to grasp.
Remember that no matter what the difficulty is,
no matter where it is, no matter who is affected,
you have no patient but yourself; you have
nothing to do but convince yourself of the truth
which you desire to see manifested."

Charles Haanel

JACK CANFIELD

*It's OK to notice what you don't want, because it gives you
contrast to say, "This is what I do want." But the fact is,
the more you talk about what you don't want, or talk about
how bad it is, read about that all the time, and then say how
terrible it is—well, you're creating more of that.*

You cannot help the world by focusing on the negative things. As
you focus on the negative events of the world, you not only add to
them, but you bring more negative things into your own life at the
same time.

When the pictures have appeared of something you do not want,
it is your cue to change your thinking and emit a new signal. If it
is a world situation, you are not powerless. You have *all* the power.
Focus on everybody being in joy. Focus on abundance of food. Give
your powerful thoughts to what is wanted. You have the ability to
give so much to the world by emitting feelings of love and well-
being, despite what is happening around you.

JAMES RAY

So many times people say to me, "Well, James, I have to be informed." Maybe you have to be informed, but you don't have to be inundated.

When I discovered The Secret I made a decision that I would not watch the news or read newspapers anymore, because it did not make me feel good. The news services and the newspapers are not in any way to blame for broadcasting bad news. As a global community, we are responsible for it. We buy more newspapers when a huge drama is the headline. The news channels' ratings skyrocket when there is a national or international disaster. So the newspapers and news services give us more bad news because, as a society, that's what we are saying we want. The media is effect, and we are cause. It is just the law of attraction in action!

The news services and newspapers will change what they deliver to us when we emit a new signal and focus on what we want.

MICHAEL BERNARD BECKWITH

Learn to become still, and to take your attention away from what you don't want, and all the emotional charge around it, and place the attention on what you wish to experience. . . . Energy flows where attention goes.

> "Think truly, and thy thoughts shall the world's famine feed."
>
> *Horatio Bonar* (1808–1889)

Are you beginning to see the phenomenal power you have in this world, just through your existence? As you focus on the good things you feel good, and you are bringing more good things to the world. At the same time, you are bringing more good things into your own life. When you feel good you uplift your life, and you uplift the world!

The law is perfection in operation.

DR. JOHN DEMARTINI

I always say, when the voice and the vision on the inside become more profound, clear, and loud than the opinions on the outside, you've mastered your life!

LISA NICHOLS

It's not your job to change the world, or the people around you. It's your job to go with the flow inside of the Universe, and to celebrate it inside the world that exists.

You are the master of your life, and the Universe is answering your every command. Don't become mesmerized by the pictures that have appeared if they are not what you want. Take responsibility for them, make light of them if you can, and let them go. Then think new thoughts of what you want, feel them, and be grateful that it is done.

The Universe Is Abundant

DR. JOE VITALE

One of the questions I get asked all the time is if everyone uses The Secret, and they all treat the Universe like a catalogue, aren't we going to run out of stuff? Won't everyone just make a run for it and bust the bank?

MICHAEL BERNARD BECKWITH

What's beautiful about the teaching of The Secret is that there's more than enough to go around for everyone.

There is a lie that acts like a virus within the mind of humanity. And that lie is, "There's not enough good to go around. There's lack and there's limitation and there's just not enough." And that lie has people living in fear, greed, stinginess. And those thoughts of fear, greed, stinginess, and lack become their experience. So the world has taken a nightmare pill.

The truth is that there's more than enough good to go around. There's more than enough creative ideas. There's more than enough power. There's more than enough love. There's more than enough joy. All of this begins to come through a mind that is aware of its own infinite nature.

To think there is not enough is to look at the outside pictures and think that everything comes from the outside. When you do that, you will most surely see lack and limitation. You now know that nothing comes into existence from the outside, and that everything first comes from thinking and feeling it on the inside. Your mind is the creative power of all things. So how can there be any lack? It's impossible. Your ability to think is unlimited, and so the things you can think into existence are unlimited. And so it is with everyone. When you truly *know* this, you are thinking from a mind that is aware of its own infinite nature.

JAMES RAY

Every great teacher who has ever walked the planet has told you that life was meant to be abundant.

> "The essence of this law is that you must think abundance; see abundance, feel abundance, believe abundance. Let no thought of limitation enter your mind."

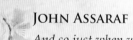

Robert Collier

JOHN ASSARAF

And so just when we think that resources are dwindling, we find new resources that can achieve the same things.

The true story of a Belize oil team is an inspiring example of the power of the human mind to bring forth resources. The directors of Belize Natural Energy Limited were trained by the eminent Dr. Tony Quinn, who specializes in Humanistic Physiology training. With Dr. Quinn's mind power training, the directors were confident that their mental picture of Belize being a successful oil-producing country would be achieved. They took a brave step forward to drill for oil in Spanish Lookout, and in one short year their dream and vision became a reality. Belize Natural Energy Limited discovered oil of the highest quality, in abundant flows where fifty other companies had failed to find any. Belize has become an oil-producing country because an extraordinary team of people believed in the unlimited power of their mind.

Nothing is limited—not resources or anything else. It is only limited in the human mind. When we open our minds to the unlimited creative power, we will call forth abundance and see and experience a whole new world.

DR. JOHN DEMARTINI

Even though we say we have lack, it's because we don't open up our vision and see all of what is around us.

DR. JOE VITALE

You know when people start to live from their heart and go for what they want, they don't go for the same things. That's the beauty of this. We don't all want BMWs. We don't all want the same person. We don't all want the same experiences. We don't all want the same clothing. We don't all want . . . (fill in the blank).

You are here on this glorious planet, endowed with this wonderful power, to create your life! There are no limits to what you can create for You, because your ability to think is unlimited! But you cannot create other people's lives for them. You cannot think for them, and if you try to force your opinions on others you will only attract like forces to You. So let all others create the life they want.

 MICHAEL BERNARD BECKWITH

There's enough for everyone. If you believe it, if you can see it, if you act from it, it'll show up for you. That's the truth.

> "If you have any lack, if you are prey to poverty
> or disease, it is because you do not believe or
> do not understand the power that is yours. It is
> not a question of the Universal giving to you.
> It offers everything to everyone—there is no
> partiality."
>
> *Robert Collier*

The Universe offers *all* things to *all* people through the law of attraction. You have the ability to choose what you want to experience. Do you want there to be enough for you and for everyone? Then choose that and know, "There is abundance of all things." "There is an unlimited supply." "There is so much magnificence." Each of us has the ability to tap into that unlimited invisible supply through our thoughts and feelings, and bring it into our experience. So choose for You, because you're the only one who can.

LISA NICHOLS

Everything that you want—all the joy, love, abundance, prosperity, bliss—it's there, ready for you to grab ahold of it. And you've got to get hungry for it. You've got to be intentional. And when you become intentional and on fire for what you want, the Universe will deliver every single thing that you've been wanting. Recognize the beautiful and wonderful things around you, and bless and praise them. And on the other side, the things that aren't currently working the way you want them to work, don't spend your energy faulting or complaining. Embrace everything that you want so you can get more of it.

Lisa's wise words, to "praise and bless" the things around you, are worth their weight in gold. Praise and bless everything in your life! When you are praising or blessing you are on the highest frequency of love. In the Bible, the Hebrews used the act of blessing to bring forth health, wealth, and happiness. They knew the power of blessing. For many people the only time they have blessed someone was when they sneezed, and so they have not used one of the greatest powers to their full advantage. The dictionary defines blessing as "invoking divine favor and conferring well-being or prosperity," so begin right now to invoke the power of blessing in your life, and bless everything and everyone. Likewise with praising, for when you are praising someone or something you are giving love, and as you emit that magnificent frequency, it will return to you a hundred-fold.

Praising and blessing dissolves all negativity, so praise and bless your enemies. If you curse your enemies, the curse will come back to harm *you*. If you praise and bless them you will dissolve all negativity and discord, and the love of the praising and blessings will return to you. As you praise and bless, you will feel yourself shift into a new frequency with the feedback of good feelings.

DR. DENIS WAITLEY

Most of the leaders in the past missed the great part of The Secret, which is to empower and share with others.

This is the best time to have ever been alive in history. It's the first time we've ever had the power to gain knowledge at our fingertips.

With this knowledge you are becoming aware—of the truth of the world, and yourself. My greatest insights into The Secret on the subject of the world came from the teachings of Robert Collier, Prentice Mulford, Charles Haanel, and Michael Bernard Beckwith. With that understanding came total freedom. I truly hope that you can come to the place of that same freedom. If you can, then through your existence and the power of your thoughts, you will bring the greatest good to this world and to the future of all humankind.

Secret Summaries

- *What you resist, you attract, because you are powerfully focused on it with emotion. To change anything, go within and emit a new signal with your thoughts and feelings.*

- *You cannot help the world by focusing on the negative things. As you focus on the world's negative events, you not only add to them, but you also bring more negative things into your own life.*

- *Instead of focusing on the world's problems, give your attention and energy to trust, love, abundance, education, and peace.*

- *We will never run out of good things because there's more than enough to go around for everyone. Life is meant to be abundant.*

- *You have the ability to tap into the unlimited supply through your thoughts and feelings and bring it into your experience.*

- *Praise and bless everything in the world, and you will dissolve negativity and discord and align yourself with the highest frequency—love.*

$= \frac{1}{2z^2}$; $I_4(2) = \frac{3}{8}\sqrt{\frac{\pi}{2^5}}$

$\Rightarrow T(\frac{1}{2}) = \sqrt{\pi}$

The Secret to You

DR. JOHN HAGELIN

When we look around us, even at our own bodies, what we see is the tip of the iceberg.

BOB PROCTOR

Think of this for a moment. Look at your hand. It looks solid, but it's really not. If you put it under a proper microscope, you'd see a mass of energy vibrating.

JOHN ASSARAF

Everything is made up of the exact same thing, whether it's your hand, the ocean, or a star.

DR. BEN JOHNSON

Everything is energy, and let me help you to understand that just a little bit. There's the Universe, our galaxy, our planet,

*and then individuals, and then inside of this body are organ
systems, then cells, then molecules, and then atoms. And then
there is energy. So there are a lot of levels to think about, but
everything in the Universe is energy.*

When I discovered The Secret, I wanted to know what science and
physics understood in terms of this knowledge. What I found was
absolutely amazing. One of the most exciting things about living
in this time is that the discoveries of quantum physics and new
science are in total harmony with the teachings of The Secret, and
with what all the great teachers have known throughout history.

I never studied science or physics at school, and yet when I read
complex books on quantum physics I understood them perfectly
because I wanted to understand them. The study of quantum physics helped me to have a deeper understanding of The Secret, on an
energetic level. For many people, their belief is strengthened when
they see the perfect correlation between the knowledge of The Secret and the theories of new science.

Let me explain how you are the most powerful transmission tower
in the Universe. In simple terms, all energy vibrates at a frequency.
Being energy, you also vibrate at a frequency, and what determines
your frequency at any time is whatever you are thinking and feeling. All the things you want are made of energy, and they are vibrating too. *Everything* is energy.

Here is the "wow" factor. When you think about what you want,
and you emit that frequency, you cause the energy of what you

want to vibrate at that frequency and you bring it to You! As you focus on what you want, you are changing the vibration of the atoms of that thing, and you are causing it to vibrate *to* You. The reason you are the most powerful transmission tower in the Universe is because you have been given the power to focus your energy through your thoughts and alter the vibrations of what you are focused on, which then magnetically draws it to you.

When you think about and feel those good things that you want, you have immediately tuned yourself to that frequency, which then causes the energy of all those things to vibrate to you, and they appear in your life. The law of attraction says that like attracts like. You are an energy magnet, so you electrically energize everything to you and electrically energize yourself to everything you want. Human beings manage their own magnetizing energy, because no one outside of them can think or feel for them, and it is thoughts and feelings that create our frequencies.

Almost one hundred years ago, without the benefit of all the scientific discoveries of the last hundred years, Charles Haanel knew how the Universe operated.

> "The Universal Mind is not only intelligence,
> but it is substance, and this substance is the
> attractive force which brings electrons together
> by the law of attraction so they form atoms;
> the atoms in turn are brought together by the
> same law and form molecules; molecules take

objective forms and so we find that the law is the creative force behind every manifestation, not only of atoms, but of worlds, of the Universe, of everything of which the imagination can form any conception."

Charles Haanel

BOB PROCTOR

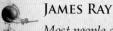

I don't care what city you're living in, you've got enough power in your body, potential power, to illuminate the whole city for nearly a week.

"To become conscious of this power is to become a 'live wire.' The Universe is the live wire. It carries power sufficient to meet every situation in the life of every individual. When the individual mind touches the Universal Mind, it receives all its power."

Charles Haanel

JAMES RAY

Most people define themselves by this finite body, but you're not a finite body. Even under a microscope you're an energy field. What we know about energy is this: You go to a quantum physicist and you say, "What creates the world?" And he or she will say, "Energy." Well, describe energy.

"OK, it can never be created or destroyed, it always was,
always has been, everything that ever existed always exists,
it's moving into form, through form and out of form." You
go to a theologian and ask the question, "What created the
Universe?" And he or she will say, "God." OK, describe God.
"Always was and always has been, never can be created or
destroyed, all that ever was, always will be, always moving
into form, through form and out of form." You see, it's the
same description, just different terminology.

So if you think you're this "meat suit" running around,
think again. You're a spiritual being! You're an energy field,
operating in a larger energy field.

How does all of this make you a spiritual being? For me, the answer to that question is one of the most magnificent parts of the
teachings of The Secret. You are energy, and energy cannot be created or destroyed. Energy just changes form. And that means You!
The true essence of You, the pure energy of You, has always been
and always will be. You can never *not* be.

On a deep level, you know that. Can you imagine not being? Despite everything you have seen and experienced in your life, can
you imagine not being? You cannot imagine it, because it is impossible. You are eternal energy.

The One Universal Mind

DR. JOHN HAGELIN

Quantum mechanics confirms it. Quantum cosmology confirms it. That the Universe essentially emerges from thought and all of this matter around us is just precipitated thought. Ultimately we are the source of the Universe, and when we understand that power directly by experience, we can start to exercise our authority and begin to achieve more and more. Create anything. Know anything from within the field of our own consciousness, which ultimately is Universal consciousness that runs the Universe.

So depending upon how we use that power, positively or negatively, that's the kind of body in terms of health, that's the kind of environment we create. So we are the creators, not only of our own destiny, but ultimately we are the creators of Universal destiny. We are the creators of the Universe. So there's no limit, really, to human potential. It's the degree to which we recognize those deep dynamics and exercise them, the degree to which we harness our power. And that really has to do again with the level at which we think.

Some of the greatest teachers and avatars described the Universe in the same way as Dr. Hagelin, by saying that all that exists is the One Universal Mind, and there is nowhere that the One Mind is not. It exists in everything. The One Mind is all intelligence, all wisdom, and all perfection, and it is everything and everywhere at the same time. If everything is the One Universal Mind, and the whole of it exists everywhere, then it is all in You!

Let me help you understand what that means for you. It means that *every possibility already exists.* All knowledge, all discoveries, and all inventions of the future, are in the Universal Mind as possibilities, waiting for the human mind to draw them forth. Every creation and invention in history has also been drawn from the Universal Mind, whether the person consciously knew that or not.

How do you draw from it? You do it through your awareness of it, and by using your wonderful imagination. Look around you for needs waiting to be filled. Imagine if we had a great invention to do this, or imagine if we had a great invention to do that. Look for the needs, and then imagine and think their fulfilment into being. You don't have to work out the discovery or the invention. The Supreme Mind holds that possibility. All you have to do is hold your mind on the end result and imagine filling the need, and you will call it into being. As you ask and feel and believe, you will receive. There is an unlimited supply of ideas waiting for you to tap into and bring forth. You hold everything in your consciousness.

"Divine Mind is the one and only reality."

Charles Fillmore

JOHN ASSARAF

We're all connected. We just don't see it. There isn't an
"out there" and an "in here." Everything in the Universe is
connected. It is just one energy field.

So whichever way you look at it, the result is still the same. We are
One. We are all connected, and we are all part of the One Energy
Field, or the One Supreme Mind, or the One Consciousness, or
the One Creative Source. Call it whatever you want, but we are all
One.

If you think about the law of attraction now, in terms of us all being
One, you will see its absolute perfection.

You will understand why your negative thoughts about someone else will return to harm only You. We are One! You cannot
be harmed unless you call harm into existence by emitting those
negative thoughts and feelings. You have been given free will to
choose, but when you think negative thoughts and have negative feelings, you are separating yourself from the One and All
Good. Think about every negative emotion there is and you will
discover that every one of them is based in fear. They come from
thoughts of separation and from seeing yourself as separate from
another.

Competition is an example of separation. First, when you have
thoughts of competition, it is coming from a lack mentality, as
you are saying there is a limited supply. You are saying there is

not enough for everybody, so we have to compete and fight to get things. When you compete you can never win, even if you think you won. By the law of attraction, as you compete you will attract many people and circumstances to compete against You in every single aspect of your life, and in the end you will lose. We are all One, and so when you compete, you compete against You. You have to get competition out of your mind, and become a creative mind. Focus only on *your* dreams, *your* visions, and take all competition out of the equation.

The Universe is the Universal supply and supplier of everything. Everything comes from the Universe, and is delivered to you *through* people, circumstances, and events, by the law of attraction. Think of the law of attraction as the law of supply. It is the law that enables you to draw from the infinite supply. When you emit the perfect frequency of what you want, the perfect people, circumstances, and events will be attracted to you and delivered!

It is not people who are giving you the things you desire. If you hold that false belief, you will experience lack, because you are looking at the outside world and people as the supply. The true supply is the invisible field, whether you call that the Universe, the Supreme Mind, God, Infinite Intelligence, or whatever else. Whenever you receive anything, remember that you attracted it to you by the law of attraction, and by being on the frequency and in harmony with the Universal Supply. The Universal Intelligence which pervades everything moved people, circumstances, and events to give that thing to you, because that is the law.

LISA NICHOLS

We often get distracted with this thing called our body and our physical being. That just holds your spirit. And your spirit is so big it fills a room. You are eternal life. You are God manifested in human form, made to perfection.

MICHAEL BERNARD BECKWITH

Scripturally we could say that we are the image and the likeness of God. We could say we are another way that the Universe is becoming conscious of itself. We could say that we are the infinite field of unfolding possibility. All of that would be true.

> "Ninety-nine percent of who you are is invisible and untouchable."
>
> *R. Buckminster-Fuller* (1895–1983)

You are God in a physical body. You are Spirit in the flesh. You are Eternal Life expressing itself as You. You are a cosmic being. You are all power. You are all wisdom. You are all intelligence. You are perfection. You are magnificence. You are the creator, and you are creating the creation of You on this planet.

JAMES RAY

Every tradition has told you that you were created in the image and likeness of the creative source. That means that you have God potential and power to create your world, and you are.

*Maybe you've created things to this point that are wonderful
and worthy of you, and maybe you haven't. The question
I'd ask you to consider is, "Are the results you have in your
life what you really want? And are they worthy of you?" If
they're not worthy of you, then wouldn't now be the right
time to change those? Because you have the power to do that.*

> "All power is from within and therefore
> under our control."
>
> *Robert Collier*

You Are Not Your Past

JACK CANFIELD

*A lot of people feel like they're victims in life, and they'll often
point to past events, perhaps growing up with an abusive
parent or in a dysfunctional family. Most psychologists
believe that about 85 percent of families are dysfunctional, so
all of a sudden you're not so unique.*

*My parents were alcoholics. My dad abused me. My
mother divorced him when I was six. . . . I mean, that's
almost everybody's story in some form or not. The real
question is, what are you going to do now? What do you
choose now? Because you can either keep focusing on that,*

or you can focus on what you want. And when people start focusing on what they want, what they don't want falls away, and what they want expands, and the other part disappears.

> "A person who sets his or her mind on the dark side of life, who lives over and over the misfortunes and disappointments of the past, prays for similar misfortunes and disappointments in the future. If you will see nothing but ill luck in the future, you are praying for such ill luck and will surely get it."
>
> *Prentice Mulford*

If you go back over your life and focus on the difficulties from the past, you are just bringing more difficult circumstances to You now. Let it all go, no matter what it is. Do it for you. If you hold a grudge or blame someone for something in the past, you are only harming You. You are the only one who can create the life you deserve. As you deliberately focus on what you want, as you begin to radiate good feelings, the law of attraction will respond. All you have to do is make a start, and as you do, you will unleash the magic.

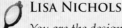

LISA NICHOLS

You are the designer of your destiny. You are the author. You write the story. The pen is in your hand, and the outcome is whatever you choose.

Michael Bernard Beckwith

The beautiful thing about the law of attraction is that you can begin where you are, and you can begin to think "real thinking," and you can begin to generate within yourself a feeling tone of harmony and happiness. The law will begin to respond to that.

Dr. Joe Vitale

So now you start to have different beliefs, like, "There is more than enough in the Universe." Or you have the belief that, "I'm not getting older, I'm getting younger." We can create it the way we want it, by using the law of attraction.

Michael Bernard Beckwith

And you can break yourself free from your hereditary patterns, cultural codes, social beliefs, and prove once and for all that the power within you is greater than the power within the world.

Dr. Fred Alan Wolf

You may be thinking, "Well, that's very nice, but I can't do that." Or, "She won't let me do that!" Or, "He'll never let me do that." Or, "I haven't got enough money to do that." Or, "I'm not strong enough to do that." Or, "I'm not rich enough to do that." Or, "I'm not, I'm not, I'm not, I'm not."

Every single "I'm not" is a creation!

It is a good idea to become aware when you say, "I'm not" and to think about what you are creating as you say it. A powerful insight shared by Dr. Wolf has been equally documented by all the great teachers with the power of the words *I am*. When you say "I am," the words that follow are summoning creation with a mighty force, because you are declaring it to be fact. You are stating it with certainty. And so immediately after you say, "I am tired" or "I am broke" or "I am sick" or "I am late" or "I am overweight" or "I am old," the Genie says, "Your wish is my command."

Knowing this, wouldn't it be a good idea to begin to use the two most powerful words, *I AM*, to your advantage? How about, "I AM receiving every good thing. I AM happy. I AM abundant. I AM healthy. I AM love. I AM always on time. I AM eternal youth. I AM filled with energy every single day."

In his book *The Master Key System*, Charles Haanel claims that there is an affirmation that incorporates every single thing any human being can want, and that this affirmation will bring about harmonious conditions to all things. He adds, "The reason for this is because the affirmation is in strict accordance with the Truth, and when Truth appears every form of error or discord must necessarily disappear."

The affirmation is this: "I am whole, perfect, strong, powerful, loving, harmonious, and happy."

If it sounds like work to drag what you want out of the invisible and into the visible, try this shortcut: see what you want as absolute *fact*. This will manifest what you want with the speed of light The second you ask, it is *fact* in the Universal spiritual field, and that field is all that exists. When you conceive something in your mind, know it is a *fact,* and that there can be no question about its manifestation.

> "There is no limit to what this law can do for
> you; dare to believe in your own ideal; think of
> the ideal as an already accomplished fact."
>
> *Charles Haanel*

When Henry Ford was bringing his vision of the motor vehicle into our world, people around him ridiculed him and thought he had gone mad to pursue such a "wild" vision. Henry Ford knew much more than the people who ridiculed him. He knew The Secret and he knew the law of the Universe.

> "Whether you think you can or think you can't,
> either way you are right."
>
> *Henry Ford* (1863–1947)

Do you think you can? You can achieve and do anything you want with this knowledge. In the past you may have underestimated how brilliant you are. Well, now you know you are the Supreme Mind and that you can draw anything you want from that One Supreme Mind. Any invention, any inspiration, any answer, anything. You can do anything you want. You are a genius beyond description, so start telling yourself that and become aware of who you really are.

MICHAEL BERNARD BECKWITH

Are there any limits to this? Absolutely not. We are unlimited beings. We have no ceiling. The capabilities and the talents and the gifts and the power that is within every single individual that is on the planet, is unlimited.

Be Aware of Your Thoughts

All your power is in your awareness of that power, and through *holding* that power in your consciousness.

Your mind can be like a runaway steam train if you let it. It can take you off to thoughts of the past, and then take you off to thoughts of the future by taking past bad events and projecting those *into* your future. Those out-of-control thoughts are creating too. When you are aware, you are in the present and you know what you are thinking. You have gained control of your thoughts, and that is where all your power is.

So how do you become more aware? One way is to *stop* and ask yourself, "What am I thinking now? What am I feeling now?" The moment you ask you are aware, because you have brought your mind back to the present moment.

Whenever you think of it, bring yourself back to the awareness of now. Do it hundreds of times each day, because, remember, all of your power is in your awareness of your power. Michael Bernard Beckwith sums up the awareness of this power when he says, "Remember to remember!" Those words have become the theme song of my life.

To help myself become more aware, so I would *remember to remember,* I asked the Universe to give me a *gentle* nudge to bring me back to the present whenever my mind has taken over and is "having a party" at my expense. That gentle nudge happens by me bumping myself or dropping something, a loud noise, or a siren or an alarm going off. All of these things are signals to me that my mind has taken off, and to come back to the present. When I receive these signals I stop immediately and ask myself, "What am I thinking? What am I feeling? Am I aware?" And of course in the moment I do that, I am aware. The very moment you ask yourself if you aware, you are there. You are aware.

> "The real secret of power is consciousness of power."
>
> *Charles Haanel*

As you become aware of the power of The Secret, and begin to use it, all of your questions will be answered. As you begin to have a deeper understanding of the law of attraction you can start to make asking questions a habit, and as you do, you will receive the answer to each one. You can begin by using this book for that very purpose. If you are seeking an answer or guidance on something in your life, ask the question, believe you will receive, and then open this book randomly. At the exact place where the pages fall open will be the guidance and answer you are seeking.

The truth is that the Universe has been answering you all of your life, but you cannot receive the answers unless you are aware. Be aware of everything around you, because you are receiving the answers to your questions in every moment of the day. The channels those answers can come through are *unlimited*. They could be delivered in the form of a newspaper headline that attracts your attention, or overhearing someone speaking, or a song on the radio, or signage on a truck passing by, or receiving a sudden inspiration. *Remember to remember*, and become aware!

I have found in my own life and in others' lives that we do not think well of ourselves or love ourselves completely. To not love ourselves can keep what we want *from* us. When we don't love ourselves, we are literally pushing things away from us.

Everything we want, whatever it may be, is motivated by love. It is to experience the feelings of *love* in having those things—youth, money, the perfect person, job, body, or health. To attract the things we love we must transmit love, and those things will appear immediately.

The catch is, to transmit the highest frequency of love, you must love yourself, and that can be difficult for many. If you focus on the outside and what you see now, you may trip yourself up, because what you see and feel about you now is the result of what you *used* to think. If you don't love you, the person you see now is likely to be full of faults that you have found in yourself.

To love yourself fully, you must focus on a new dimension of You. You must focus on the *presence* inside of you. Take a moment and sit still. Focus on feeling the *life presence* inside You. As you focus on the *presence* within, it will begin to reveal itself to You. It is a feeling of pure love and bliss, and it is perfection. That *presence* is the perfection of You. That *presence* is the *real* You. As you focus on that presence, as you feel, love, and praise that presence, you will love yourself fully, quite possibly for the first time in your life.

Any time you look at yourself with critical eyes, switch your focus immediately to the *presence* within, and its perfection will reveal itself to You. As you do this, all imperfections that have manifested in your life will dissolve, because imperfections cannot exist in the light of this presence. Whether you want to regain perfect eyesight, dissolve disease and restore well-being, turn poverty into abundance, reverse aging and degeneration, or eradicate any negativity, focus on and love the presence within you and perfection will manifest.

> "The absolute truth is that the 'I' is perfect
> and complete; the real 'I' is spiritual and can
> therefore never be less than perfect; it can never
> have any lack, limitation, or disease."
>
> *Charles Haanel*

Secret Summaries

- *Everything is energy. You are an energy magnet, so you electrically energize everything to you and electrically energize yourself to everything you want.*

- *You are a spiritual being. You are energy, and energy cannot be created or destroyed—it just changes form. Therefore, the pure essence of you has always been and always will be.*

- *The Universe emerges from thought. We are the creators not only of our own destiny but also of the Universe.*

- *An unlimited supply of ideas is available to you. All knowledge, discoveries, and inventions are in the Universal Mind as possibilities, waiting for the human mind to draw them forth. You hold everything in your consciousness.*

- *We are all connected, and we are all One.*

- *Let go of difficulties from your past, cultural codes, and social beliefs. You are the only one who can create the life you deserve.*

- *A shortcut to manifesting your desires is to see what you want as absolute fact.*

- *Your power is in your thoughts, so stay aware. In other words, "Remember to remember."*

The Secret to Life

NEALE DONALD WALSCH

AUTHOR, INTERNATIONAL SPEAKER, AND SPIRITUAL MESSENGER

There is no blackboard in the sky on which God has written your purpose, your mission in life. There's no blackboard in the sky that says, "Neale Donald Walsch. Handsome guy who lived in the first part of the twenty-first century, who . . ." And then there's a blank. And all I have to do to really understand what I'm doing here, why I'm here, is to find that blackboard and find out what God really has in mind for me. But the blackboard doesn't exist.

So your purpose is what you say it is. Your mission is the mission you give yourself. Your life will be what you create it as, and no one will stand in judgment of it, now or ever.

You get to fill the blackboard of your life with whatever you want. If you have filled it in with baggage from the past, wipe it clean. Erase everything from the past that does not serve you, and be grateful it brought you to this place now, and to a new beginning. You have a clean slate, and you can start over—right here, right now. Find your joy and live it!

JACK CANFIELD

It took a lot of years for me to get this point, because I grew up very much with this idea that there was something I was supposed to do, and if I wasn't doing it, God wouldn't be happy with me.

When I really understood that my primary aim was to feel and experience joy, then I began to do only those things which brought me joy. I have a saying: "If it ain't fun, don't do it!"

NEALE DONALD WALSCH

Joy, love, freedom, happiness, laughter. That's what it is. And if you just experience joy sitting there and meditating for an hour, by golly, do that. If you experience joy eating a salami sandwich, then do that!

JACK CANFIELD

When I pet my cat I'm in a state of joy. When I walk in nature I'm in a state of joy. So I want to constantly put myself in that state, and when I do, then all I have to do is have the intention of what I want, and what I want manifests.

Do the things that you love and that bring you joy. If you don't know what brings you joy, ask the question, "What is my joy?" And as you find it and commit yourself to it, to joy, the law of attraction will pour an avalanche of joyful things, people, circumstances, events and opportunities into your life, all because you are radiating joy.

DR. JOHN HAGELIN

So inner happiness actually is the fuel of success.

Be happy *now*. Feel good *now*. That's the only thing you have to do. If that's the only thing you get from reading this book, then you have received the greatest part of The Secret.

DR. JOHN GRAY

Anything that makes you feel good is always going to be drawing in more.

You are reading this book right now. It's you that drew this into your life, and it's your choice whether you want to take it and utilize it, if it feels good. If it doesn't feel good, then let it go. Find something that feels good, that resonates with your heart.

The knowledge of The Secret is being given to you, and what you do with it is entirely in your hands. Whatever you choose for You is right. Whether you choose to use it, or whether you choose not to use it, you get to choose. The freedom of choice is yours.

> "Follow your bliss and the universe will open
> doors for you where there were only walls."
>
> *Joseph Campbell*

LISA NICHOLS

When you follow your bliss you live in a constant space of joy. You open yourself to the abundance of the Universe. You're excited to share your life with those you love, and your excitement, your passion, your bliss become contagious.

DR. JOE VITALE

That's what I'm doing almost all the time—following my excitement, my passion, my enthusiasm—and I'm doing it throughout my day.

BOB PROCTOR

Enjoy life, because life is phenomenal! It's a magnificent trip!

MARIE DIAMOND

You will live in a different reality, a different life. And people will look at you and say, "What do you do different from me?" Well, the only thing that is different is that you work with The Secret.

MORRIS GOODMAN

And then you can do and have and be things that people once said that's impossible for you to do and have and be.

DR. FRED ALAN WOLF

We're really now moving into a new era. It's the era where the last frontier is not space, as "Star Trek" would say, but it's going to be Mind.

DR. JOHN HAGELIN

I see a future of unbounded potential, unbounded possibilities. Remember we're using, at most, 5 percent of the potential of the human mind. One hundred percent human potential is the result of proper education. So imagine a world where people are using their full mental and emotional potential. We could go anywhere. We could do anything. Achieve anything.

This time on our glorious planet is the most exciting time in history. We are going to see and experience the impossible becoming possible, in every field of human endeavor and on every subject. As we let go of all thoughts of limitation, and *know* that we are unlimited, we will experience the limitless magnificence of humankind, expressed through sport, health, art, technology, science, and every single field of creation.

Embrace Your Magnificence

BOB PROCTOR

See yourself with the good that you desire. Every religious book tells us that, every great book on philosophy, every great leader, all the avatars who have ever lived. Go back and study

*the wise ones. Many of them have been presented to you in
this book. They all understood one thing. They understood
The Secret. Now you understand it. And the more you use it,
the more you'll understand it.*

The Secret is within you. The more you use the power within you,
the more you will draw it to you. You will reach a point where you
won't need to practice anymore, because you will Be the power,
you will be the perfection, you will Be the wisdom, you will Be the
intelligence, you will Be the love, you will Be the joy.

LISA NICHOLS

*You've come to this juncture in your life, merely because
something in you kept saying, "You deserve to be happy."
You were born to add something, to add value to this world.
To simply be something, bigger and better than you were
yesterday.*

*Every single thing you've been through, every single moment
that you've come through, were to all prepare you for this
moment right now. Imagine what you can do from this day
forward with what you now know. Now you get that you are
the creator of your destiny. So how much more do you get
to do? How much more do you get to be? How many more
people do you get to bless, simply by your mere existence?
What will you do with the moment? How will you seize the
moment? No one else can dance your dance, no one else can
sing your song, no one else can write your story. Who you
are, what you do, begins right now!*

MICHAEL BERNARD BECKWITH

I believe that you're great, that there's something magnificent about you. Regardless of what has happened to you in your life. Regardless of how young or old you think you might be. The moment you begin to "think properly," this something that's within you, this power within you that's greater than the world, it will begin to emerge. It will take over your life. It will feed you. It will clothe you. It will guide you, protect you, direct you, sustain your very existence. If you let it. Now that is what I know, for sure.

The earth turns on its orbit for You. The oceans ebb and flow for You. The birds sing for You. The sun rises and it sets for You. The stars come out for You. Every beautiful thing you see, every wondrous thing you experience, is all there, for You. Take a look around. None of it can exist, without You. No matter who you thought you were, now you know the Truth of Who You Really Are. You are the master of the Universe. You are the heir to the kingdom. You are the perfection of Life. And now you know The Secret.

May the joy be with you!

> "The secret is the answer to all that has been, all that is, and all that will ever be."
>
> *Ralph Waldo Emerson*

Secret Summaries

- *You get to fill the blackboard of your life with whatever you want.*

- *The only thing you need to do is* feel good *now.*

- *The more you use the power within you, the more power you will draw through you.*

- *The time to embrace your magnificence is now.*

- *We are in the midst of a glorious era. As we let go of limiting thoughts, we will experience humanity's true magnificence, in every area of creation.*

- *Do what you love. If you don't know what brings you joy, ask, "What is my joy?" As you commit to your joy, you will attract an avalanche of joyful things because you are radiating joy.*

- *Now that you have learned the knowledge of The Secret, what you do with it is up to you. Whatever you choose is right. The power is all yours.*

Biographies

JOHN ASSARAF

A former street kid, John Assaraf is now an international bestselling author, lecturer, and business advisor, committed to helping entrepreneurs create greater wealth while living an extraordinary life. John has dedicated the last twenty-five years to researching the human brain, quantum physics, and business strategies, as they relate to achieving success in business and life. By applying what he learned, John has built four multi-million-dollar companies from scratch, and he now shares his unique business-building and moneymaking ideas with entrepreneurs and small business owners worldwide. To learn more, visit www.onecoach.com.

MICHAEL BERNARD BECKWITH

In 1986 Dr. Beckwith, a nonaligned, trans-religious progressive, founded the Agape International Spiritual Center, whose membership numbers 10,000 locally and hundreds of thousands of friends and affiliates worldwide. He serves on international panels with spiritual luminaries such as His Holiness the Dalai Lama; Dr. A. T. Ariyaratne, founder of Sarvodaya; and Arun Gandhi, grandson of Mohandas K. Gandhi. He is co-founder of the Association for Global New Thought, whose annual conference brings together scientists, economists, artists, and spiritual leaders at the cutting edge of guiding humanity to its highest potential.

Dr. Beckwith teaches meditation and scientific prayer, conducts retreats, and speaks at conferences and seminars. He is the originator of the Life Visioning Process, and author of *Inspirations of the Heart*, *40 Day Mind Fast Soul Feast*, and *A Manifesto of Peace*. Please go to www.Agapelive.com for more information.

GENEVIEVE BEHREND
(c. 1881–c. 1960)

Genevieve Behrend studied with the great Judge Thomas Troward, one of the early teachers of spiritual metaphysics, and author of *Mental Science*. Thomas Troward chose Behrend as his only pupil, and she went on to teach, lecture, and practice "mental science" in North America for thirty-five years, as well as write her own popular books, *Your Invisible Power* and *Attaining Your Heart's Desire*.

LEE BROWER

Lee Brower is the founder and CEO of Empowered Wealth, an international consulting firm that offers businesses, foundations, families, and individuals systems and solutions for empowering their Core, Experience, Contribution, and Financial Assets. He is also the founder of The Quadrant Living Experience, LLC, a boutique firm that licenses and trains an international network of Quadrant Living Advisors. Lee is co-author of *Wealth Enhancement and Preservation* and author of *The Brower Quadrant*. His two websites are www.empowered wealth.com and www.quadrantliving.com.

JACK CANFIELD

Jack Canfield, author of *The Success Principles™*, is the co-creator of the phenomenal number one *New York Times* bestselling *Chicken Soup for the Soul®* series, which currently has more than 100 million copies in print. He is America's leading expert in creating success breakthroughs for entrepreneurs, corporate leaders, managers, sales professionals, employees, and educators, and has helped hundreds of thousands of individuals achieve their dreams. For more information on Jack Canfield, visit www.jackcanfield.com.

ROBERT COLLIER (1885–1950)

Robert Collier was a prolific and hugely successful American writer. All of his books, which include *The Secret of the Ages* and *Riches within Your Reach*, were founded on Collier's own extensive research into metaphysics and on his personal belief that success, happiness, and abundance are easily and rightfully attainable by everyone. The excerpts contained in this book were taken from the seven-volume set *The Secret of the Ages*, with the generous consent of Robert Collier Publications.

DR. JOHN F. DEMARTINI
D.C., B.SC.

Once told he was learning disabled, John Demartini is now a doctor, philosopher, author, and international speaker. For many years he had a successful chiropractic clinic, and was once named Chiropractor of the Year. Dr. Demartini is now a consultant to health professionals, and speaks and writes on the subjects of healing and philosophy. His personal transformation methodologies have helped thousands of people find a greater order and happiness in their lives. His website is www.drde martini.com.

MARIE DIAMOND

Marie is an internationally known Feng Shui master who has been practicing for more than twenty years, refining the knowledge given to her at an early age. She has advised numerous Hollywood celebrities, major film directors and producers, music giants, and famous authors. She has helped many well-known public figures create more success in all areas of their lives. Marie created Diamond Feng Shui, Diamond Dowsing, and Inner Diamond Feng Shui to bridge the law of attraction in an individual's environment. Her website is www.mariediamond .com.

MIKE DOOLEY

Mike is not a "career" teacher or speaker; instead, as a "life adventurer" he has successfully navigated both the corporate and entrepreneurial arenas. After living and working around the world for Price Waterhouse, in 1989 he co-founded Totally Unique Thoughts (TUT) to retail and wholesale its own line of inspirational gifts. From the ground up, TUT grew into a regional chain of stores, was carried by every major U.S. department store, and reached consumers around the globe through distribution centers in Japan, Saudi Arabia, and Switzerland, selling over one million Totally Unique T-shirts®. In 2000 he transformed TUT into a web-based inspirational and philosophical Adventurers Club, which now has over 60,000 members from more than 169 countries. He is the author of a number of books, including three volumes of *Notes from the Universe* and the internationally acclaimed audio program, *Infinite Possibilities: The Art of Living Your Dreams.* You can learn more about Mike and TUT at www.tut.com.

BOB DOYLE

Bob Doyle is the creator and facilitator of the Wealth Beyond Reason program, a powerful multi-media curriculum on the law of attraction and its practical application. Bob focuses on the science of the law of attraction to help you more purposefully activate the law in your life, and to attract wealth, success, awesome relationships, and anything else you desire. For more information, visit www.wealthbeyondreason.com.

HALE DWOSKIN

Author of the *New York Times* bestseller *The Sedona Method*, Hale Dwoskin dedicates himself to freeing people of limiting beliefs in order to help them achieve whatever their hearts desire. The Sedona Method is a unique and powerful technique that shows you how to release limiting and painful feelings, beliefs, and attitudes. Hale has taught these principles to corporations and individuals worldwide for the past thirty years. His website is www.sedona.com.

MORRIS GOODMAN

Dubbed "The Miracle Man," Morris Goodman made headlines in 1981 when he recovered from horrific injuries after crashing his airplane. He was told he would never walk, speak, or function normally again, but today Morris travels the world inspiring and uplifting thousands of people with his astounding story. Morris's wife, Cathy Goodman, is also featured in *The Secret*, telling her own inspiring account of self-healing. To learn more, visit www.themiracleman.org.

JOHN GRAY, PH.D.

John Gray is the author of *Men Are from Mars, Women Are from Venus*, the number one best-selling relationship book of the last decade, selling over thirty million copies. He has authored fourteen other bestsellers, and conducts seminars for thousands of participants. His focus is to help men and women understand, respect, and appreciate their differences, in both personal and professional relationships. His new book is *The Mars and Venus Diet and Exercise Solution*. To learn more, visit www.marsvenus.com.

CHARLES HAANEL (1866–1949)

Charles Haanel was a successful American businessman and the author of several books, all of which contained Haanel's own ideas and methods that he used to achieve greatness in his own life. His most famous work is *The Master Key System*, which gives twenty-four weekly lessons to greatness, and is as popular today as it was when it was first published in 1912.

JOHN HAGELIN, PH.D.

Dr. John Hagelin is a world-renowned quantum physicist, educator, and public policy expert. His book, *Manual for a Perfect Government,* explains how to solve major societal and environmental problems and create world peace through policies in harmony with the laws of nature. John Hagelin was awarded the prestigious Kilby Award, which recognizes scientists who have made major contributions to society. He was also the Natural Law Party presidential candidate in 2000. John is regarded by many as one of the greatest scientists on the planet today. His website is www.hagelin.org.

BILL HARRIS

Bill Harris is a professional speaker, teacher, and business owner. After studying ancient and modern research about the nature of the mind and transformational techniques, Bill created Holosync, an audio technology that results in the benefits of deep meditation. His company, Centerpointe Research Institute, has enabled thousands of people worldwide to lead happier, stress-free lives. To find out more, visit www.centerpointe.com.

DR. BEN JOHNSON
M.D., N.M.D., D.O.

Originally trained in Western medicine, Dr. Johnson became interested in energy healing after overcoming a life-threatening illness using unconventional methods. He is chiefly interested in The Healing Codes, a form of healing discovered by Dr. Alex Lloyd. Today Dr. Johnson and Alex Lloyd run The Healing Codes Company, which distributes the teachings. Visit www.healingcodes.com to learn more.

LORAL LANGEMEIER

Loral Langemeier is the founder of Live Out Loud, which provides financial education and support to help people reach their monetary goals. She believes that mindset is the key to building wealth, and has assisted many people in becoming millionaires. Loral speaks to individuals and corporations, passing on her knowledge and expertise. Her website is www.liveoutloud.com.

PRENTICE MULFORD (1834–1891)

Prentice Mulford was one of the earliest writers and founders of the New Thought movement, and was a recluse for much of his life. He has influenced countless writers and teachers with his work, which deals with mental and spiritual laws. Titles include *Thoughts Are Things* and *The White Cross Library*, a collection of his many essays.

LISA NICHOLS

Lisa Nichols is a powerful advocate of personal empowerment. She is the founder and CEO of Motivating the Masses and Motivating the Teen Spirit, two comprehensive skills programs that work to bring about profound change in the lives of teenagers, women, and entrepreneurs, as well as provide services to the educational system, corporate clients, empowerment organizations, and faith-based programs. Lisa is the co-author of *Chicken Soup for the African American Soul*, from the best-selling worldwide series. Her website is www.lisa-nichols.com.

BOB PROCTOR

Bob Proctor's wisdom came to him through a lineage of great teachers. It began with Andrew Carnegie who passed it to Napoleon Hill, and then Hill passed it to Earl Nightingale. Earl Nightingale then passed the torch of wisdom to Bob Proctor. Bob has worked in the area of mind potential for over forty years. He travels the globe teaching The Secret, helping companies and individuals to create lives of prosperity and abundance through the law of attraction. He is the author of the international bestseller, *You Were Born Rich*. To learn more about Bob, visit www.bobproctor.com.

JAMES ARTHUR RAY

A student of the principles of true wealth and prosperity his entire life, James developed The Science of Success and Harmonic Wealth®, which teaches people how to receive unlimited results in all areas: financially, relationally, intellectually, physically, and spiritually. His personal performance systems, corporate training programs, and coaching aids are utilized worldwide, and he speaks regularly on the subjects of true wealth, success, and human potential. James is also an expert on many Eastern, indigenous, and mystical traditions. Visit his website at www.jamesray.com.

DAVID SCHIRMER

David Schirmer is a highly successful share trader, investor, and investment trainer who conducts workshops, seminars, and courses. His company, Trading Edge, teaches people how to create unlimited income by developing a mindset that is conducive to wealth. Schirmer's analysis of the Australian and overseas share and commodity markets is held in high regard due to his regular accuracy. To learn more, visit www.tradingedge.com.au.

MARCI SHIMOFF, MBA

Marci Shimoff is co-author of the enormously successful *Chicken Soup for the Woman's Soul* and *Chicken Soup for the Mother's Soul*. She is a transformational leader who speaks passionately about personal development and happiness. Her work is specially geared toward enhancing women's lives. She is also co-founder and president of The Esteem Group, a company that offers self-esteem and inspirational programs for women. Her website is www.marcishimoff.com.

DR. JOE VITALE, MSC.D.

Joe Vitale, homeless twenty years ago, is now considered to be one of the top marketing specialists in the world. He has written numerous books concerning principles of success and abundance, including *Life's Missing Instruction Manual*, *Hypnotic Writing*, and *The Attractor Factor*, all number one bestsellers. Joe holds a doctorate degree in Metaphysical Science and is a certified hypnotherapist, metaphysical practitioner, ordained minister, and Chi Kung healer. Visit www .mrfire.com to learn more.

DR. DENIS WAITLEY, PH.D.

Dr. Waitley is one of America's most respected authors, lecturers, and consultants on high-performance human achievement. He was employed to train NASA astronauts, and later implemented the same program with Olympic athletes. His audio album, *The Psychology of Winning*, is the all-time bestselling program on self-mastery, and he is also the author of fifteen non-fiction books, including several international bestsellers. His website is www.waitley.com.

NEALE DONALD WALSCH

Neale Donald Walsch is a modern-day spiritual messenger and the bestselling author of the groundbreaking three-book *Conversations with God* series, which broke all records on the *New York Times* bestsellers list. Neale has published twenty-two books, as well as video and audio programs, and travels the world carrying the message of a New Spirituality. He may be contacted at www.nealedonald walsch.com.

WALLACE WATTLES (1860–1911)

American-born Wallace Wattles spent many years studying various religions and philosophies before he began to write about the practice of "New Thought" principles. Wattles's many books have had a significant impact on today's prosperity and success teachers. His most famous work is the prosperity classic *The Science of Getting Rich*, published in 1910.

FRED ALAN WOLF, PH.D.

Fred Alan Wolf is a physicist, writer, and lecturer, with a doctorate in theoretical physics. Dr. Wolf has taught at universities throughout the world, and his work in quantum physics and consciousness is well known through his writing. He is the author of twelve books, including

Taking the Quantum Leap, which won the National Book Award. Today Dr. Wolf continues to write and lecture throughout the world, and carry out his fascinating research into the relationship of quantum physics and consciousness. Visit his website, www .fredalanwolf.com.

Afterword: Ten Secret Insights

These are the ten most life-changing insights I have had over the last ten years of practicing and living The Secret every day. They can make manifesting your desires easier than ever before, eliminate struggles and suffering, and help you reach a level of peace and joy that you might never have felt before.

1. YOUR REACTION TO WHAT HAPPENS IN YOUR LIFE DICTATES WHAT HAPPENS NEXT

Reactions are powerful creators because they contain every element needed to manifest—they're a combination of thought, belief, and feeling *in action*. Positive reactions create more positive things, and negative reactions create more negative things. If you can respond to negative situations calmly and lightly, instead of with emotional turbulence, what happens next in your life will be so much better.

2. NEGATIVE THOUGHTS ARE NOT TRUE

Only our *belief* in negative thoughts makes them appear to be true to us; at their very core, negative thoughts are just that—thoughts. But when we believe negative thoughts they become the root cause of all unhappiness.

Make it a golden rule of your life not to believe a single negative thought, and your life will be absolutely magnificent!

3. LETTING GO ALLOWS FOR MANIFESTATION

If there's something you want to manifest but nothing's happening, it could be because you're feeling resistant to the fact that you don't have it yet. You're still creating, but you're creating the *absence* of what you want. To change what you're creating and allow for manifestation, let go—be genuinely okay with *not* getting what you want. Let go and get on with your life, and whatever it is you want will have a much easier path to you.

4. IF YOU'RE SUFFERING OR STRUGGLING AT ANY TIME, IT'S BECAUSE YOU'RE BELIEVING A STORY THAT ISN'T TRUE

While pain is a physical phenomenon in our world, suffering comes from our mind. Suffering is the result of believing a story about a situation or about a person that isn't true, which means that if you stop telling the story, suffering will stop. A negative story that makes you suffer is a fabrication of the mind, and when you can see that clearly you will stop believing it, and you will stop attracting evidence of it being true. Change your mind now, and then your world will change!

5. DON'T BE IN CONFLICT WITH ANYONE OR ANYTHING

Opposing, fighting, or struggling against anything or anyone in life causes conflict. Conflict attracts more conflict; fighting against something attracts more things to fight against, and struggle attracts more things to struggle over. Step away from conflict, because when you're in conflict with *anyone* or *anything* in life, it harms *you*.

6. NOTHING STAYS THE SAME—TOMORROW THINGS WILL BE DIFFERENT

Everything is energy, and the nature of energy is that it's constantly changing. Knowing this, you can count on the fact that if there's something disturbing your peace of mind, it will pass. If you stop giving *any attention* to what's disturbing you, tomorrow things will be different—without you doing a single thing.

7. DON'T RESIST NEGATIVE EMOTIONS

Don't fight or resist negative emotions, because your resistance will hold them to you. Negative emotions are simply a movement of energy, and if you allow them to be without resisting them—without giving them the time of day—they will pass by quickly.

8. THE FEWER OPINIONS YOU HAVE, THE FEWER CONCLUSIONS YOU COME TO, AND THE FEWER FIXED IDEAS YOU HOLD TO, THE MORE BLISS AND JOY WILL BE YOURS

Opinions, conclusions, and fixed ideas are judgments formulated by the mind. They're a subtle negative act. We've been conditioned to believe that if we have opinions about all the things that are "bad" or "wrong" we're a good person. But it's the person who has the fewest opinions—the person who judges the least—who has bliss and joy and countless good things in their life.

9. RESISTANCE CAUSES SUFFERING. ALLOWANCE ELIMINATES SUFFERING.

You are resisting when you push against a situation or a person with thoughts like "I don't like it," "I don't want it," "I'm not happy with that person," "This shouldn't have happened." The greater your resistance, the greater the suffering—and the more you cement the circumstance to you. Your *allowance* of the same circumstance eliminates suffering immediately, and allows the circumstance to change!

10. BE AWARE, AND BE HERE NOW

Stop listening to the endless commentary and chatter of your mind. Instead, be aware, and be here now. When you're walking down the street, *be on* the street, and not listening to the narration in your head. When you're traveling in a car, *be in* the car, and not lost in the thoughts in your head. When someone is talking to you, *listen* to them; focus on what they're saying, and stop listening to the commentary inside your head. Here and now, right where you are, there are no thoughts, no problems, and no suffering—there is only joy.

May The Secret bring you love and
joy for your entire existence.

That is my intention for you,
and for the world.

For more information, visit www.thesecret.tv.